EYE ON
Art

FOLK ART

by Tina Kafka

LUCENT BOOKS
A part of Gale, Cengage Learning

GALE
CENGAGE Learning

Detroit • New York • San Francisco • New Haven, Conn • Waterville, Maine • London

This book is dedicated to the librarians
of the San Diego Public Library.

© 2008 Gale, a part of Cengage Learning

For more information, contact
Lucent Books
27500 Drake Rd.
Farmington Hills, MI 48331-3535
Or you can visit our Internet site at gale.cengage.com

LIBRARY OF CONGRESS CATALOGING-IN-PUBLICATION DATA

Kafka, Tina, 1950-
  Folk art / by Tina Kafka.
    p. cm. -- (Eye on art)
  Includes bibliographical references and index.
  ISBN 978-1-59018-960-3 (hardcover)
  1. Folk art--Juvenile literature. I. Title.
  N5313.K34 2007
  745--dc22
                                                                2007021292

ISBN-10:1-59018-960-4

Printed in the United States of America
2 3 4 5 6 7 12 11 10 09 08

CONTENTS

Foreword

"Art has no other purpose than to brush aside . . . everything that veils reality from us in order to bring us face to face with reality itself."
—French philosopher Henri-Louis Bergson

Some 31 thousand years ago, early humans painted strikingly sophisticated images of horses, bison, rhinoceroses, bears, and other animals on the walls of a cave in southern France. The meaning of these elaborate pictures is unknown, although some experts speculate that they held ceremonial significance. Regardless of their intended purpose, the Chauvet-Pont-d'Arc cave paintings represent some of the first known expressions of the artistic impulse.

From the Paleolithic era to the present day, human beings have continued to create works of visual art. Artists have developed painting, drawing, sculpture, engraving, and many other techniques to produce visual representations of landscapes, the human form, religious and historical events, and countless other subjects. The artistic impulse also finds expression in glass, jewelry, and new forms inspired by new technology. Indeed, judging by humanity's prolific artistic output throughout history, one must conclude that the compulsion to produce art is an inherent aspect of being human, and the results are among humanity's greatest cultural achievements: masterpieces such as the architectural marvels of ancient Greece, Michelangelo's perfectly rendered statue of *David*, Vincent van Gogh's visionary painting *Starry Night*, and endless other treasures.

The creative impulse serves many purposes for society. At its most basic level, art is a form of entertainment or the means for a satisfying or pleasant aesthetic experience. But art's true power lies not in its potential to entertain and delight but in its ability to enlighten, to reveal the truth, and by doing so to uplift the human spirit and transform the human race.

One of the primary functions of art has been to serve religion. For most of Western history, for example, artists were paid by the church to produce works with religious themes and subjects. Art was thus a tool to help human beings transcend mundane, secular reality and achieve spiritual enlightenment. One of the best-known, and largest-scale, examples of Christian religious art is the Sistine Chapel in the Vatican in Rome. In 1508 Pope Julius II commissioned Italian Renaissance artist Michelangelo to paint the chapel's vaulted ceiling, an area of 640 square yards (535 sq. m). Michelangelo spent four years on scaffolding, his neck craned, creating a panoramic fresco of some three hundred human figures. His paintings depict Old Testament prophets and heroes, sibyls of Greek mythology, and nine scenes from the Book of Genesis, including the Creation of Adam, the Fall of Adam and Eve from the Garden of Eden, and the Flood. The ceiling of the Sistine Chapel is considered one of the greatest works of Western art and has inspired the awe of countless Christian pilgrims and other religious seekers. As eighteenth-century German poet and author Johann Wolfgang von Goethe wrote, "Until you have seen this Sistine Chapel, you can have no adequate conception of what man is capable of."

In addition to inspiring religious fervor, art can serve as a force for social change. Artists are among the visionaries of any culture. As such, they often perceive injustice and wrongdoing and confront others by reflecting what they see in their work. One classic example of art as social commentary was created in May 1937, during the brutal Spanish civil war. On May 1 Spanish artist Pablo Picasso learned of the recent attack on the small Basque village of Guernica by German airplanes allied with fascist forces led by Francisco Franco. The German pilots had used the village for target practice, a three-hour bombing that killed sixteen hundred civilians. Picasso, living in Paris, channeled his outrage over the massacre into his painting *Guernica*, a black, white and gray mural that depicts dismembered animals and fractured human figures whose faces are contorted in agonized expressions. Initially, critics and the public condemned the painting as an incoherent hodgepodge, but the work soon came to be seen as a powerful anti-war statement and remains an iconic symbol of the violence and terror that dominated world events during the remainder of the twentieth century.

The impulse to create art—whether painting animals with crude pigments on a cave wall, sculpting a human form from marble, or commemorating human tragedy in a mural—thus serves many purposes. It offers an entertaining diversion nourished the imagination and the spirit, decorates and beautifies the world, and chronicles the age. But underlying all these functions is the desire to reveal that which is obscure—to illuminate, clarify and perhaps ennoble. As Picasso himself stated, "The purpose of art is washing the dust of daily life off our souls."

The Eye on Art series is intended to assist readers in understanding the various roles of art in society. Each volume offers an in-depth exploration of a major artistic movement, medium, figure or profession. All books in this series are beautifully illustrated with full-color photographs and diagrams. Riveting narrative, clear technical explanation, informative sidebars, fully documented quotes, a bibliography, and a thorough index all provide excellent starting points for research and discussion. With these features, the Eye on Art series is a useful introduction to the world of art—a world that can offer both insight and inspiration.

Introduction

Diverse Art with Common Features

Folk art occupies a unique place in the world of art. It encompasses many different types of objects made of different materials using different techniques by people of every culture. A quilt made in New York, a basket in Africa, a carousel in Mexico, and an embroidered blouse in Cambodia are all considered folk art. And yet, as diverse as it is, all folk art has one feature in common: The people who make it have not been formally trained in artistic style or technique. Additional features also help to define folk art and distinguish it from other forms of creative expression. Traditionally, folk art is made from materials that are readily available and easily accessible to the folk artist. Long ago that meant that folk art was created only from natural materials such as plants, shells, stones, or animal parts. Though this still may be the case, present day folk artists may also have access to common materials that have been mass-produced, such as synthetic yarns and plastic. They might use these materials, however, in unexpected ways. Folk art is one way that people adapt to the various demands of their environment. The demands may be physical, such as the need for food and shelter, or they may be spiritual or social. Humans have always gathered in groups for various reasons. They gather to create communities. They gather to celebrate. They gather to play. Folk art is often an important part of social occasions. It is a way for people to create common experiences. The folk art that is part of social occasions communicates subtly, but always offers important clues about the values and personality of a culture.

As the world becomes more global and cultures become less isolated, it is common to find folk art from distant cultures distributed around the world. Sometimes the purpose of a particular form of folk art changes to meet new needs in an increasingly fast-paced and complex world. In his book *Folk Art of Latin America*, Marion Oettinger, Jr., explains:

> Traditional folk painters in Haiti once painted delightfully telling pictures of their daily and ritual lives for themselves, but began exporting them when healthy markets appeared in Paris, New York, and elsewhere. Today they are being called on to paint Haitian public health posters and billboards warning of the dangers of AIDS and other threats.[1]

Folk art, such as these African water gourds, is created by people who are not formally trained in artistic style or technique.

In many cultures today, people also find it more practical to create folk art to sell to tourists or for export to other countries, using the proceeds to purchase basic living necessities or raw materials to sustain their art.

Like the work of trained artists, some examples of all types of folk art are considered more beautiful than others. In the last century, folk art has begun to be appreciated like the work of formally trained artists. Many people collect folk art, specializing in the form that captures their interest. One collector may love fine quilts and another may search for handmade wooden spoons. The finest examples of folk art are displayed in museums. Sometimes entire museums are devoted to the study and exhibition of folk art, such as the American Folk Art Museum in New York City.

The Roots
of Folk Art

The roots of folk art are twofold. People have always created objects to help ease the tasks of daily living. For example, shards of pottery, remnants of baskets, and carefully carved tools attest to age old needs to carry water, store food, and improve the chances of a successful hunt. Moreover, as anthropologists sift through artifacts of ancient cultures, they find evidence that these objects were often decorated in ways that did not change their function at all. Decoration did not make a clay pot hold more water or make a stone carving tool sharper. In all cultures, people decorated the objects they used in their daily lives, and this provides evidence of a universal human tendency to want to make things beautiful. Folk art, therefore, is found in all cultures. Ten thousand years ago, as groups of people learned to cultivate food and domesticate animals, they became less nomadic, or wandering. Since they no longer had to pack their belongings and move with the seasons or follow the herds of animals they hunted, they settled into more permanent communities. And, as they settled down, they acquired more possessions. These possessions, which today are unearthed from ancient Egyptian tombs and excavated from Native American shelters, provide evidence of this universal human tendency to decorate and embellish the objects used in daily life.

Furthermore, each culture developed unique designs to decorate these objects. The natural talents of the artists, their cultural traditions, climate and geography all influenced the designs. Because of this, anthropologists can easily distinguish pottery of ancient Greece or individual Indian tribes, for example, solely by studying the composition of the clay used and the unique style of decoration.

In 13th and 14th century Europe, some artists formed guilds with specific rules and regulations that governed the designs and materials used to make each object. The guilds trained artists in what were considered the proper and best artistic techniques. The concept of guilds then traveled to North America with European colonists and became part of American society as the colonies grew and prospered. Some people believe that the first American folk artists were craftsmen who were not members of a guild at all, but possessed a flair for both a craft and a sales pitch. These traveling craftsmen roamed the countryside looking for customers. They did not necessarily have the finest tools or the best materials, but their work (the paintings, woodcarvings, signs, toys, needlework, and other handmade objects) helped explain what was important to the ordinary people who lived long ago in early America.

Naming the Art

It was not until about one hundred years ago that people in the United States became interested in collecting and studying these objects and arguing about what to call them. The term "folk art" was coined in Europe, where it referred to handmade objects used in the homes, religious ceremonies, and the personal adornment of peasants. These close-knit communities shared common lifestyles. Furthermore, their households, clothing, and the items they used in their daily lives and religious ceremonies had many common features. Throughout the 20th century, the term that is used to refer to the paintings, sculpture, furniture, and textiles created by folk artists has changed many times. Each change reflects a subtle difference in the way that these artists and their work are viewed by society. By studying the collection of the American Folk Art Museum in New York City, it is possible to follow the progression of terms for "folk art" in this country. In the early part of the 20th century, the creators of these objects were labeled "self-taught," in order to distinguish them from artists who had received formal art training. As years went by and tastes changed, the art was known as "primitive," "naïve," and "folk" art. Some of these terms, such as "folk art," faded from fashion only to regain popularity a few years later. The term "outsider" art was popularized in the 1980s to refer to art created by prisoners or people living in mental institutions. Later, outsider art referred to art made by any artist who was not formally trained. Some people object to that term altogether, since it implies a judgment about these particular artists. As Brooke Davis Anderson explains in *American Anthem*, "This

Folk art pieces, such as these 19th century American dolls, reflect the cultural traditions of a particular community.

arguably divisive terms suggests 'otherness'—after all, who is in, who is out?"[2] For that reason, the American Folk Art Museum avoids this term completely, though it is still widely used elsewhere.

In recent years, the term "vernacular art" has gained favor in the world of folk art collectors and museums. "Vernacular" refers to an object or a term that is native to a particular place. Some people prefer this term because it implies that the makers of folk art identify with a particular community, usually the community in which they were born and raised.

The Importance of Folk Art

Today, the terms folk art, vernacular art, and self-taught art are used interchangeably. More important than the name, however, is the role this art plays in people's lives. The authors of *Folk Art in American Life* explain its importance in this country: "Folk art has permeated and enhanced American life, from bedroom to barroom, from kitchen to cradle, from park to prairie, from graveyard to barnyard, from ship to shore, from colonial days until today."[3] These objects, though used for common household tasks, were more than common tools. A quilt that is considered an example of folk art was more than a blanket for a cold night. Though the pattern might be traditional, the fabrics used could be especially interesting. For example, the stitches might be unusually fine and the color combination particularly striking.

People in the United States were not the first, however, to recognize the importance and value of folk art. In the early 20th century, Soetsu Yanagi, a professor of folk art in Japan, coined the term *mingei* meaning "arts of the people" from two Japanese words: *min* (people) and *gei* (art). Yanagi and others feared that as society became increasingly mechanized and fragmented, the traditions of making handmade objects would be lost. Yanagi believed that the true test of a man's artistic sensibility was not whether he possessed valuable works by famous artists, but whether the objects he used in his daily life were beautiful.

These handcrafted, traditional blankets from Peru are examples of folk art that have a functional purpose in the home.

Although he founded the Japanese Folk Art Society in 1931, his campaign to preserve folk art was not realized until 1950. That year, Japan passed the Cultural Properties Protection Law. Japan's respect for folk artists is reflected in the part of that law that honors its most revered folk artists with the title "Living National Treasure." Living National Treasures receive annual financial support, and their work is exhibited throughout the world.

As the beauty and expressiveness of folk art were recognized in other countries, folk art enthusiasts in the United States began to focus more attention on it too. A small group of folk art devotees met in Richmond, Virginia, in 1987 and formed a club, which they named The Folk Art Society of America, hoping to bring the attention of Americans to world folk art. The Folk Art Society quickly became a national organization. Its focus was the documentation, preservation, study, and exhibition of folk art and folk artists from around the world. In order to encourage the continuation of folk art tradition, the group emphasized the work of contemporary folk artists. A statement in the original *Folk Art Messenger,* the group's official publication, immediately addressed the ongoing debate about what to call folk art:

> We have no intention of entering into the great folk art debate among folklorists, art historians, material culture proponents, folk-life experts, collectors, artists, folk craftsmen, aestheticians or whatever. Rather, we would propose to bring various groups under one loosely structured umbrella, sharing and discussing ideas and information, not limiting the scope or the definition of folk art. These definitions will evolve with time; the parameters of our individual study and interests will define themselves. The main idea is to get people together, to form a network of people across the United States who are basically interested in the same thing, even if they call it by a different name.[4]

The Folk Art Society continues to be an important force in the study of the world's folk art.

Popular Folk Art Designs

Despite spirited discussions of what to call it, most cultural historians agree that it is possible to learn much about a place by examining the designs or motifs that embellish its folk art. Motifs symbolizing certain ideas or values appear repeatedly in

folk art. In *American Anthem*, the curators point to symbols of American liberty in folk culture to explain, that

> The inspiration for folk art often is tied to critical moments in America's history, especially times of war or national celebration, and to an individual's personal response to those events. Symbols of liberty, for instance, became part of the common language as soon as there was an independent nation to applaud.[5]

Patriotic symbols appear commonly in quilts, folk paintings, textiles, weathervanes, toys, and many other forms of American folk art. As soon as the bald eagle became the official national emblem of the United States in 1782, it became a common motif in American folk art, as did Lady Liberty and the stars and stripes of the American flag. The popularity of these images tends to increase at times of national crises, such as wars. They become a common language that brings comfort and connection

THE HEART MOTIF IN FOLK ART

The heart is a folk motif common to many cultures. This symbol for affection has been embroidered, painted, carved, molded, and cut out of paper to decorate costumes and embellish household objects all across Europe and the United States for centuries. The Scandinavians were especially fond of the heart motif, and it is still a popular Christmas decoration in Scandinavian countries. Heart-shaped butter molds, cookie cutters, and waffle irons were common in early American kitchens. Blacksmiths often twisted the ends of metal tools and utensils into heart-shaped handles. And of course, St. Valentine's Day has been celebrated on February 14 since the 1800s by exchanging cards and candy decorated with hearts. No one knows exactly how that particular shape came to be called a "heart" since it does not resemble a human heart at all. The color of the heart, however, is almost always red, which suggests blood and high emotion in many cultures.

to the people. In fact, these curators claim that American folk art is patriotic by its very nature. Folk art reflects many things that Americans value: individual expression, freedom, ingenuity, creativity, and the fact that anything is possible in this land of golden opportunity.

Folk art motifs often cross national boundaries, however. Wars, religion, immigration, geography, and climate are important factors in the distribution of folk art motifs throughout the world. The spread of Christianity throughout Europe, for example, is responsible for motifs common to many countries. The sheep, the peacock, and the five-pointed star are common folk art motifs, and all have religious significance. The American colonists brought these religious symbols with them when they immigrated to North America.

The folk art of many countries in the world also incorporates similar secular, or non-religious, motifs. The heart, for example, is carved and shaped into furniture, household tools, and pottery all across Europe, Scandinavia, and North America. The pineapple is a sign of hospitality, the rooster represents pride, the stag symbolizes a gentle nature, and the owl symbolizes wisdom. These are all folk motifs that occur repeatedly in Europe and the Americas. The folk man and woman are worldwide symbols of marriage, varying only in the clothing that decorates their figures.

Early Native American motifs that depict the animals and plants important to their cultures can be seen in baskets, cloth, paintings, and carvings. Countries of the Eastern part of the world, including China, Japan, India, and Southeast Asia, have developed their own icons or symbols that appear in the folk art from those regions. In Japan, images of flowers that bloom at different times of the year represent the four seasons. The peony symbolizes spring, the lotus symbolizes summer, the chrysanthemum symbolizes fall, and plum blossoms symbolize winter.

Who is Anon?

The names of the artists who painted, decorated, built, stitched, and embellished folk art with motifs are often unknown. Folk art in museums, therefore, commonly bears the signature "anonymous" or "anon" in the place where an artist's name traditionally appears. There are several reasons for this anonymity. First, much of what collectors now consider folk art was never intended as such. People made tools to use in their homes and workshops, painted portraits of their friends and families, or stitched needlework to practice their sewing. Parents made toys and dolls for their children. Farmers depended on weathervanes to predict the weather. Cooks needed kitchen tools, and Native American dancers needed masks for their ceremonies. When their art was created, it was intended to serve a specific purpose, not to be displayed in a museum or collected by folk art enthusiasts.

Moreover, folk artists were often poor. Some hoped to sell their work to others to raise money for their families. Others made things in their spare time or as gifts for family and friends. Formally trained artists who hoped to gain fame and fortune from their art usually sign their work. But folk artists working outside the mainstream had no such pretensions and so did not consider their creations worthy of a signature. They were simply making beautiful objects that could be used in daily life because it gave them pleasure to do so or helped them to eke out a living.

However, even though the names of these artists are often unknown today, it is important to remember that at the time the folk art was produced, the opposite was true. Folk scholars Robert Bishop and Jacqueline Atkins explain:

> Whether the artists created only for their own pleasure to satisfy some elementary need within themselves, or whether they worked for an audience of friends, or whether they used their skills to support themselves, it should be remembered that their work was not anonymous when it was first made. Family, friends, and employers knew very well who made the work; it was art made by the people and for the people—and it was appreciated as such.[6]

Folk artists were mothers, fathers, aunts, uncles, and grandparents. They were workers and farmers. They were neighbors and

Much of the folk art housed in museums today, such as this 19th century painting of George Washington, was created by unknown, or anonymous, artists.

friends. Those who came in contact with what is now known as folk art usually knew exactly who to thank for creating it.

Folk Art of Yesterday and Today

When Soetsu Yanagi founded the Folk Art Society in Japan in the 1930s, he insisted that the artists within the society remain anonymous. This was a way to ensure that attention would be focused solely on the handmade objects themselves. However, in light of modern times and modern communication, this insistence on anonymity has become impractical and unrealistic. Folk art enthusiasts now focus more on the importance of maintaining the essence of folk art itself. And now, as always,

Sculptor Simon Rodia built the folk art environment known as Watts Towers over the course of thirty-three years.

arguments abound about how to define folk art and how to characterize that essence.

As times change and people's sensibilities change, old ideas change too in order to remain meaningful. In an industrialized world, the need to make everyday objects from available resources is less important. It is easier and faster, and often less expensive in many parts of the world, to buy cooking tools, clothing, farm implements, and toys. Yet, the human need to invent and create still exists. People still enjoy and appreciate beauty, humor, and the unexpected.

Recognizing that the nature of modern times in the mid-20th century was changing folk art, the founding curator of the American Folk Art Museum in New York, Herbert W. Hemphill, Jr., insisted on changing the boundaries of folk art. Rather than limiting folk art to work that reflected long-standing traditions and the creation of everyday

Statues made of broken glass and other discarded materials are a part of Nek Chand's Rock Garden.

objects, he broadened its definition. This new focus on individual expression can be seen clearly in the quilts of Rosie Lee Tompkins, an African-American quilt maker who died in 2006. Ms. Tompkins used bright colors and vibrant geometric shapes arranged in surprising ways. She did not limit her materials to traditional cottons but freely used rayon, velvet, fake fur and even old feed sacks to create her designs. Tompkins's quilts with their novel fabrics and designs leaped outside old boundaries. Folk art, like these quilts, that uses new and old materials in new ways has become accepted and appreciated in the last several decades.

Sometimes entire folk art environments have been created using materials that other people throw away. A folk art

Photographer Seymour Rosen celebrated the unusual, the quirky, the eccentric, and the extreme. Rosen's life changed forever in 1952 when he first glimpsed the Watts Towers, a folk art sculpture built by Simon Rodia in Los Angeles. He was so impressed that he vowed to document and preserve as many folk art environments as possible. He was fascinated by people who expressed their passion by building or painting for no reason other than they got started creating art one day and just kept on going. In his book *In Celebration of Ourselves*, Rosen writes,

> The towers are made of bar metal, which Simon bent by hand, using the nearby railroad tracks as a vise. The metal was overlapped; wrapped by hand with wire and enclosed in cement. The cement also held the tiles, seashells, pieces of glass and embossments with which Simon embellished his work. Not a single bolt, weld or rivet holds the towers together. Simon didn't know he was making engineering breakthroughs, didn't know what hadn't been done or what some people thought couldn't be done—he just needed to do something and get some acknowledgment from people.

Rosen died in 2006.

Seymour Rosen, *In Celebration of Ourselves*. San Francisco: California Living Books, 1979, p. 14.p

environment is a large-scale immoveable construction that consists of many parts and often sprawls over a large area. Simon Rodia's Watts Towers in Los Angeles are a prime example. The towers, built over a thirty-three-year period (1921–1954), consist of seventeen structures, two of which are nearly one hundred feet high. Steel pipes and rods form their foundations. Then, thousands of shards of broken glass, bottles, porcelain, seashells, and even entire bed frames are embedded in the foundations as decoration.

Folk art environments are not limited to this country. Nek Chand's Rock Garden in Chandigarh, India, is the world's largest folk art environment. Like the Watts Towers, the Rock Garden is constructed of objects that were thrown away such as broken dishes, concrete, and stones. Chand then sculpted these discards into mythological animals and imaginative figures of people. Carl Lindquist, a photographer, describes this architectural wonder:

> Built of industrial waste and thrown-away items, it is perhaps the world's most poignant and salient statement of the possibility of finding beauty in the unexpected and accidental. It expresses the fragility of the environment, the need for conservation of the earth's natural resources, the importance of balancing industrial development and sound environmental practices.[7]

Paths wind around these sculptures, and streams and waterfalls soften the effects of these stark figures made of rubble.

Perhaps the most important lesson to be learned from the similarity of these two folk environments separated by geography, culture, customs, and traditions is that folk art celebrates what is universal about the human condition. Both Nek Chand in India and Simon Rodia in California used their imaginations and creative energy to build monuments that are testimony to the importance of beauty, new ideas, and concern for the fate of the world.

2

Useful Objects of Everyday Life

The world is diverse. People of many ethnic origins, cultures, religions, and nationalities populate its mountains, valleys, plains, and deserts. But though the world is diverse, people everywhere share the tradition of making beautiful objects to use in their daily lives. Though the materials used to make these objects differ according to available resources, folk art from every culture reflects important information about the nature and personality of that culture. One way to understand the essence of a culture, is to study its folk art, which is often an honest and heartfelt expression of the ideals that a culture most values.

Pottery Helps Explain Cultures

The clay pot is one such household object. Pottery has always inspired folk artists, no matter where they have gathered to cook, carry water, and eat their food. Like all folk art, pottery reflects the important values of a culture as well as its accessible materials. The determination and strength of German settlers to North America in the 1600s, for example, is reflected in the cherished pieces of sturdy, salt-glazed stoneware that they carried with them to their new homes. These household objects with their familiar forms and designs helped the settlers feel connected to the land and traditions they left behind. This popular pottery was identified by its thick, pitted surface created by throwing salt on the clay while it was baking in the kiln, a special oven used for firing clay. Bottles, jugs, and crocks made in this way held liquids without leaking and were often used for holding drinks such as milk or beer. Until the American Revolution, immigrants brought most of their pottery to America from their previous homes. After the Revolution, however, it was considered patriotic to use American clays, which were plentiful. This pottery was often decorated with colored glazes made from local pigments. Red ware, yellow ware, and mocha ware were all forms of glazed pottery that were popular in the United States. One type of red ware, called *sgraffito*, was especially popular among German settlers to the Pennsylvania region. This technique involved scratching a floral design—usually tulips—into a wet, creamy coat that covered the finished pottery. Since tulips were a common motif in German folk art, this pottery was commonly called "tulip ware." German settlers were also able to duplicate their beloved salt-glazed stoneware in their adopted homeland.

This stoneware dish is one piece created by the influential Japanese folk potter Shoji Hamada.

The pottery traditions of Japan reflect that culture's emphasis on simplicity, balance, strength, and usefulness. The work of potter Shoji Hamada (1894–1978), renowned for creating strong simple forms, is a good example. Hamada's pottery was influenced by the work of potters from Mashiko, Japan, a center for the production of pottery for everyday use in the 1920s. Anonymous potters there shaped teapots, bowls, and other

The Pottery of Juan Quezada of Mata Ortiz, Mexico

Spencer MacCallum, an anthropologist, brought the pottery of Juan Quezada of Mata Ortiz, Mexico, to the attention of the world in the 1960s, bringing fame to both Quezada and the town. The Public Broadcasting System's *Frontline* reporter Macarena Hernandez interviewed MacCallum about Quezada's artwork:

Hernandez: Some people might think that the story of Mata Ortiz is a fairy tale—how a small town in the middle of the desert was revived by pottery.

MacCallum: I often say it's a fairy tale . . . pointing out how many fairy tales start with a desperately poor young woodcutter; and that's just the way it was with Juan. He would cut and gather firewood in the hills above the village. He loaded it on the family donkey—called Minuto, because he was so small—and carried the firewood down from the mountain. Then, he'd con his brothers and sisters into selling it door-to-door because he was so painfully shy. So, here is the tale of Juan, who is essentially illiterate today but who has brought enormous change to his village, who has made the world a more beautiful place and who has been awarded the Premio Nacional de los Artes, which is the highest honor Mexico can give a living artist. So, yes, it is a fairy tale.

PBS, "The Ballad of Juan Quezada," May, 2005, http://www.pbs.org/frontlineworld/stories/mexico403/anthropologist.html.

common household objects in simple styles. In the book *The Enduring Crafts of Japan*, Masataka Ogawa explains that Hamada was inspired by Mashiko's pottery. Ogawa wrote,

He saw here an opportunity to express in his own work the basic virtues of folk art displayed in the work of the anonymous Mashiko craftsmen: honesty, fortitude, and vigor. Hamada's style is unmistakably his own, but it is deeply rooted in Mashiko traditions. It is masculine, forthright, and bold, and those who know his work can never be taken in by mere copies of it.[8]

As one of the most famous and influential folk potters of the 20th century, Hamada's work was popular and widely imitated. He was named a Living National Treasure in Japan in 1955.

Baskets Help Carry Traditions

Though separated by geography, culture, and language, the folk art of a small religious group in the United States bears a remarkable similarity to the folk art of Japan. The United Society of Believers in Christ's Second Appearing, commonly known as the Shakers, flourished from New England to Indiana in the late 18th and early 19th centuries. Like the Japanese emphasis on simplicity, the Shakers believed that material possessions should be simple, functional, and humble without ornamentation. The Mingei International Museum of World Folk Art in San Diego once featured an exhibit of the folk art of Japan and the Shakers

Though simple in design, Shaker baskets are crafted to be strong and functional.

to highlight the similarities of these widely diverse cultures. In the prologue to the exhibition catalog entitled *Kindred Spirits: the Eloquence of Function in American Shaker and Japanese Arts of Daily Life*, June Sprigg writes. "As a group, the Shakers loved usefulness, simplicity, cleanliness, and order in everything given to them by God, which they believed to be everything, indeed, from their chairs to their souls."[9] Shaker baskets were featured prominently in the exhibition. The Shaker women, called Sisters, wove their baskets to create patterns that reflected the Shaker emphasis on simplicity. The men, or Brothers, provided and prepared the raw wood, which was mostly ash, used to make the baskets. When wood supplies became scarce, the Shakers concentrated on creating cheese or curd baskets. These small, hexagonal, open-weave baskets were used to separate the curd from the whey when making cheese and required less raw wood than did larger baskets. Shaker baskets also demonstrate first-hand how folk art from various cultures often combines to create new traditions. Though the Shakers brought their religious convictions originally from England, they adapted their ideas to basket-making techniques learned from the Algonquin Indians with whom they traded.

Most Native American groups in North America used baskets to carry and store food and household items. Apache Indians, a nomadic tribe, for example, made lightweight baskets that could be carried easily. The Pima and Papago Indians made baskets from yucca and willow, plants native to their homeland in the arid Southwest. Indians of the northwest coast, such as the Haida and Tlingit, on the other hand, wove baskets from the wood and bark of spruce and cedar trees that thrived in those cool, wet climates. Baskets made of split spruce root were so finely woven that they were watertight and could be used for cooking. The baskets were filled with water. Then rocks heated in the fire were dropped into the baskets until the water boiled. As in every form of folk art, some baskets stand out as especially beautiful. It may be the basket maker's choice of colors, texture, design, or some combination of those qualities that result in a finished basket that is particularly beautiful.

A woman carries
on the tradition
of basket-weaving
in the African nation
of Sudan.

In some cultures, baskets serve other functions. The women
of the Bolgatanga district of Northern Ghana, for example,
sell their baskets for needed income. Artisans skilled in basket
making techniques twine and twist native savannah grasses dyed
in contrasting colors into bold, alternating geometric designs.
The sturdy basket handles are woven in coordinating colors.
The shape makes these baskets ideal for carrying goods to and
from the market and for household storage. Since the African
economies are largely depressed, traditions such as basket
making are in danger of disappearing. Many artisans live on less

than one dollar per day. In an attempt to create a larger market for these baskets and preserve the traditions of these artisans, an organization called eShopAfrica offers many forms of folk art for sale on the Internet. In this way, African folk art reaches a wider market, which improves the chances that young artisans will learn the techniques and continue these folk art traditions.

Baskets provide a good illustration of the way that an object's intended use determines its finished shape. In describing baskets made by Native Americans and settlers, Rebecca Sawyer-Fay writes,

> Invariably, a basket featured a logical design; the weave and shape—and the size of the handle, bottom, and edges—were governed by the weight and type of objects the piece was to hold. A tobacco basket, for examples, had an open weave necessary for drying large leaves. Nut and berry baskets, by contrast, were small and densely woven to preserve moisture. Large splint baskets were used for carrying heavier loads, such as apples, potatoes, and corn.[10]

Baskets used for carrying fragile eggs and easily bruised fruit were often formed with raised centers to keep their ingredients safely cradled between the basket's center and sides. In Japan, special long, narrow baskets that hold flower stems are shaped to use in the art of ikebana, or flower arranging. Every culture passes its basket making traditions from one craftsman to another, using techniques, materials, and styles for many generations. The most outstanding baskets are valued for their superior craftsmanship and that difficult-to-define blend of form and function, the spirit that characterizes the best folk art.

Spoons, Bowls, and Kitchen Tools

People have also expressed their desire to beautify the objects used in daily life by decorating and embellishing the tools they used to prepare and serve food. Carved wooden spoons, for example, are a common folk tool from many cultures, especially where wood is plentiful. This used to be especially true in northern climates, where winter brought shorter periods of daylight, and farmers were forced to stay indoors for long stretches of time. They often used this time whittling small wooden objects, such as spoons or other kitchen tools. In Sweden, wood carvers filled their days making sewing imple- ments as well as kitchen utensils. A Scandinavian man displayed his intention to marry by carving a spoon that he then wore protruding from his pocket in the presence of his intended bride. Sawyer-Fay notes that even simple kitchenware can express the human impulse to make something beautiful. She writes,

> Something as basic and practical as a wrought-iron toasting fork, for example, still might be made beauti- ful with a handle worked into a scroll or heart shape. Similarly, a wooden bowl became a work of art rather than a piece of mundane kitchenware when hand- crafted from a piece of wood chosen for its distinctive grain and polished to a deep sheen.[11]

An Eskimo wood- carver turned what could have been an ordinary wood bowl into a piece of folk art by carving it into the shape of a bird and decorating it with seeds and paint.

The number of wooden kitchen tools and utensils owned by a family, called treen, from the Anglo-Saxon plural for tree, was one way to determine that family's fortune.

Europe and North America, however, are not the only sources of folk art for the kitchen. Folk artists in every culture combine fine craftsmanship, appreciation for the raw materials, and individual expression to create objects to help prepare and serve the meals. Folk artists in Mexico carve gourds made from the fruit of the calabash tree into bottles and bowls. These large gourds are frequently decorated with the ancient Aztec symbol of an eagle holding a snake, part of Mexico's national emblem. Gourd containers were used in the region as early as 8,000 B.C. Chocolate drinks are popular in Mexico, and many folk artists carve and decorate chocolate stirrers, which may have been introduced to Mexico from Spain. The decorative head of the stirrer is placed into the drink and the handle is twirled quickly between the palms, mixing the chocolate powder with the liquid.

Quilts: Staying Warm Around the World

Just as everyone needs to prepare meals, staying warm at night is priority for rich and poor all over the world. A quilted bedcover retains warmth, and though the details of quilting styles vary widely, the art of quilting itself has a long international history. Requiring only the simplest tools, such as a needle, thread, and scissors, quilts nonetheless may be one of the best-known folk arts. Quilts have been documented in ancient Egypt and China,

A patchwork quilt is created with the help of many hands.

The AIDS (Acquired Immune Deficiency Syndrome) Memorial Quilt is believed to be the largest piece of community folk art in the world. Each square of this fifty-four-ton quilt is a personal artistic memorial to one of the 91-thousand victims who have died of AIDS in the last twenty years. The quilt is the object of a battle between the Names Project Foundation, which raises money to continue the project and care for the quilt, and others who want the quilt to reflect the changing international and racial focus in the battle against AIDS. The last time the massive quilt was displayed in its entirety was in 1996 on the National Mall in Washington, D.C., when more than one million people had a chance to see it. If the quilt were unfurled today, it would cover six city blocks, according to the *New York Times*. Like all folk art, the AIDS quilt combines tradition and personal expression. Sometimes a project made by many hands becomes a source of conflict when passionate ideas clash and traditions begin to change over time.

The AIDS Memorial Quilt on the Mall in Washington, D.C.

but the quilting tradition has spread throughout the world and throughout time. Quilting has assumed new forms, employed new materials, and expressed new ideas with each stop along the way.

Quilting itself describes the process of sandwiching three layers—a decorative top, a middle layer or batting often made of wool or cotton, and a backing that is usually coordinated with the top in some way. The three layers are then stitched together, or quilted. The stitching itself can be either simple parallel rows or quite elaborate and finely detailed. Quilted fabric makes clothing warm and gives heft, or thickness, to bed covers, rugs, and wall hangings.

Quilt tops vary widely. Some quilt tops use appliqué, in which colorful fabrics are sewn on top of a background fabric. Hawaiian quilts use appliqué in dramatic patterns that are firmly entrenched in the folk art of that region. Quilts from Provence, France, derive their major interest from the stitching itself. Quilt tops from Provence are often quite simple, perhaps a single piece of solid or flowered fabric. Like much folk art, quilting styles in France reflected social and political trends. While Napoleon Bonaparte ruled France, quilt stitching featured formal garlands of laurel, puffed diamonds, and flowers within geometric shapes. Quilts made during the period known as the Second Empire (1852–1870) were filled with images of fruits, flowers, birds, initials, dates, and hearts. The random arrangement of these designs reflected the decline of the nobility and mirrored the informal lifestyle of the common people.

Though French women were fond of stitching elaborate patterns to decorate their quilts, the concept of patchwork never became popular there. French women did not see the wisdom of cutting cloth into small pieces only to sew the small pieces together again. In contrast, patchwork quilting made sense in young America, since it required thrift, utility, creativity, and resourcefulness. Patchwork quilting, however, was not a new concept. In fact, one of the oldest surviving examples of patchwork is an Egyptian canopy quilt from 980 B.C., which hangs in the Egyptian Museum in Cairo. That quilt is constructed from squares of dyed gazelle leather and decorated with ancient symbols. American colonists and westward-bound settlers in covered wagons, however, raised the art of patchwork to new heights. Making a patchwork quilt top was a way for pioneer women to turn leftover fabric and worn-out clothing into warm blankets for cold winter nights and pass the time during long westward journeys.

Patchwork quilts were practical for other reasons too. Women, who found themselves far from their homes and families, sought the companionship of others in the same situation.

A Gee's Bend, Alabama, quilter stands in front of her quilt at the exhibit "The Quilts of Gee's Bend," held at the Museum of Fine Arts in Houston.

Quilting brought people together, as groups of women gathered in quilting "bees" to stitch their patchwork quilt tops to the two other layers that completed a quilt. In this way, too, patchwork patterns traveled through communities and along the Westward trails. The names of patterns also changed as they traveled. One popular pattern, "Bear Paw," which had meaning on the edge of the forest in the Wild West, was changed to "Duck's Foot in the Mud," when muddy roads posed more hazards to settlers than wild bears. The pattern "Jacob's Ladder" in New England was called "Stepping Stones" in Virginia, "Tail of Benjamin's Kite" in Pennsylvania, "Wagon Tracks" in Mississippi, and "Underground Railroad" in Kentucky.

Quilts, like all folk art, reflected the values and lifestyles of the people who made them. The Amish, who take joy in simple pleasures, make quilts well known for their bright colors and simple patterns. The quilts made by the African-American women of Gee's Bend, Alabama, a small community isolated by a bend in the Alabama River, developed a quilting style similar to that of the Amish. Using bright colors and simple geometric patterns, the quilters of Gee's Bend continue the quilting tradition begun by their ancestors, who were slaves on the cotton plantations. In 2002, the Museum of Fine Arts in Houston, organized an exhibition of the Gee's Bend Quilts that traveled to twelve cities in the United States. The following year, the Gee's Bend Quilters' Collective began marketing quilts made by the fifty living Gee's Bend quilters. Each quilt is unique and signed by its maker.

Rugs: Folk Art Underfoot

Since quilts and rugs share many features, it is perhaps not surprising that the earliest surviving quilted object is a rug. According to a quilt history timeline compiled by the International Quilt Study Center at the University of Nebraska, a quilted linen carpet found in a Mongolian cave dates from the 2nd century A.D. That ancient quilted object is housed in the Institute of Archaeology in Leningrad, Russia. Another early

rug is the famous Pazyryk carpet, which was discovered in a tomb in Siberia. Believed to be from the 5th century B.C., the Pazyryk carpet was preserved in permafrost until it was discovered in 1949.

Rugs have been documented since ancient times. But they became a folk art only after they moved from palace floors in the Far, Near, and Middle East to the simple floors of the common people in Europe and the New World. American settlers used their initiative to create rugs that are considered distinctly American.

Rugs in the United States were woven, braided, and hooked with simple tools and available materials. The introduction of burlap in the 1820s, the coarse fabric used to hold bags of seeds and grain, inspired a great surge in the popularity of rug hooking. Burlap was easy to use as a backing material and widely available. Sawyer-Fay notes that hooked rugs are firmly entrenched in the folk art of America:

This example of a nineteenth-century American hooked rug demonstrates how folk art can be functional and decorative in the home.

Essentially paintings in fabric, hooked rugs offer vivid, highly personal interpretations of time-honored themes. Farm animals and flowers, stylized geometrics, storybook characters, and even the family dog achieved immortality in the hands of talented 'hookers,' as makers of these richly colored and textured textiles are known.[12]

Hooked rugs were not the only rugs made from worn out clothing, however. Braided rugs were also popular. Braided rugs provided another way to use worn out clothing and scraps of fabric. Short strips of fabric were sewn together, and the resulting long strips were then braided and sewn into a circular or oval rug. As in all forms of folk art, unique color combinations, striking patterns produced by varying fabrics, or unusually skilled braid work resulted in rugs that stand out as especially beautiful. The best examples are collected and exhibited in museums.

Rugs and quilts, household tools, baskets, and pottery are all forms of folk art that demonstrate the value people place on making the objects beautiful that they use in their daily lives. There are of course many other everyday objects that testify to this universal human tendency. Decoration can be seen on everything from cookie cutters to writing implements, tools used to shoe horses and harvest grain, hold candles, or sweep floors. Throughout history and across all cultures, it has been important to people to express their individual creativity and personal vision by decorating the objects they use to carry out even the most mundane tasks.

3

Ready-to-Wear

People usually devote great care and attention to the clothing they wear, whether it is worn to work every day or reserved for special occasions. Clothing reflects how people view themselves in terms of their community, whether they fit in or feel outside the mainstream. Likewise, clothing often communicates position or status. Most cultures have developed particular styles of clothing and certain garments that distinguish one culture from another. Clothing, therefore, is an ideal medium for folk art. It provides a visible way to express the ideas, images, and values that a culture deems important.

The Folk Wear of South America

The Andes Mountains slice from north to south through South America, dividing the continent into four geographical regions: mountains, valleys, coast, and the Amazon basin. This geography isolates groups of people, causing vast cultural differences that have persisted for thousands of years. These differences are evident in the unique styles and techniques of making and decorating clothing that have developed over the centuries. And within those styles and techniques, some stand out. The most beautiful examples, those that use the materials in a way that embodies their best qualities, help express the unique and special attributes of each culture.

Native people occupied South America for thousands of years before Spanish explorer and conqueror Francisco Pizarro, lured by the gold and riches of the Incas, invaded the region. The arrival of the Spanish and other Europeans changed South America in profound ways. Not only did Pizarro find gold, other minerals, and thickly wooded forests, he found a land rich in artistic traditions. But these traditions changed with the onrush of new influences from Europe, as styles and traditions became a mixture of old and new. Lucy Davies and Mo Fini, who specialize in the study of handicrafts of South America, write that:

Despite everything, artistic traditions evolved in numerous ways, absorbing new methods, concepts and

In Peru, the woven belt, or chumpi, plays a large role in many folk traditions. Here, a woman weaves a chumpi.

materials while maintaining ancient techniques and symbols. Although much was lost, a creative process occurred: old and new co-existed and at times combined to produce the variety found in the Americas today, incorporating both the native and more popular traditions.[13]

Long-held traditions of weaving cloth in the Andes Mountains were among those that withstood the Spanish invasion most effectively.

The Wayuu Indians of La Guajira in northeast Colombia managed to retain many old weaving traditions, despite the Spanish invasion. The Wayuu have a saying that indicates the importance of weaving in their culture: "Ser mujer es saber tejer," or "To be a woman is to know how to weave."[14] Weaving is not only a way to make cloth in many parts of the Andes, it also carries both social and spiritual significance. In some isolated villages high in the Andes, the women still wear the traditional aksu, a skirt of two pieces of woven cloth that overlap at the sides and are held up by a belt. An aksu is sometimes worn alone with a shirt or blouse or can be worn as a second layer of clothing like an apron. In either case, it is held in place with a belt. Belts, or chumpi, play an important role in South American clothing that goes beyond holding up pants and skirts. Many folk traditions are expressed using this simple item of clothing. Some communities near Cuzco, Peru's capital, still place chumpis on certain mountaintops. Each chumpi is believed to carry a coded message to the gods. In some parts of Peru, women traditionally give birth lying on a chumpi and then wrap their newborn in a chumpi to ensure the baby's good health. The Incas of Peru, in fact, are given the most credit for preserving the ancient designs that continue to be incorporated into their woven belts.

Both woven belts and knitted objects are often decorated with traditional images, such as pumas, llamas, the planet Venus, fish, ducks and a two-headed snake. In fact, every piece of textile from a specific community traditionally bore the same symbols and colors. This custom was a source of pride and identity.

Davies and Fini explain that these symbols were important because,

> Each piece also carried its specific symbols, and each symbol told a story. In the Andean world, for example, the planet Venus (Chaska) played an important role in mythology and in the agricultural pattern. Its appearance was used to forecast the coming year's rainfall, vital for sowing and harvest time. This symbol and that of the sun (Inti) predominated in textile decoration.[15]

The backstrap loom, pictured, is still used today by the Mayans and other culture groups to weave intricately patterned cloth.

Traditional Clothing in Mexico

Mexican traditional clothing, like that of Mexico's southern neighbors, is also a rich combination of native Indian and Spanish designs. When the Spanish conquered the Mayan Indians of Mexico in the 1500s, many textile traditions from

Spain were incorporated into existing Mayan folk techniques used to decorate clothing. The Mayan Indians considered the weaving of cloth to be a sacred duty. According to ancient Mayan tradition, at the beginning of the world the Goddess of the Moon taught women to weave sacred designs to use for their clothing. This cloth, along with the tools and materials used to make it are still considered sacred.

In Chiapas, one area of Mexico, cloth is still woven on a backstrap loom. The construction of a backstrap loom is simple, but the special designs, known as brocade, which are woven on the loom are complex. The loom itself consists of two sticks or rods that hold the long threads, or warp, that form the foundation of the woven piece. A rope connected to the stick farthest from the weaver's body can be tied around any post or tree. The other stick is connected to a strap that then goes behind the weaver's body. The weaver controls the tightness of the loom's threads by leaning against the strap. Brocade involves adding extra threads to the cross threads, the weft, as the foundation cloth is being woven, which results in raised designs. Many of the brocade designs still woven survive from pre-Columbian times. They portray gods, saints, and animals that protect the growth of corn and ensure the fertility of the earth. Women who master these designs are greatly admired in their villages.

Brocade cloth is still used to make many traditional Mexican garments. Women and men both wear the huipil, a sleeveless garment made with brocade panels. This simple garment is constructed from a rectangle or square piece of cloth with a hole in the center. The cloth is then folded in half and stitched up the sides, leaving armholes. Elaborate designs are sometimes embroidered around the neck and sleeve edges. Women wear the huipil over a skirt while men wear them with loose pants held by a woven belt. In the mountain areas of Chiapas, men and women also wear a cape or shawl known as a tzute, although the men's tzutes are decorated more simply than those of the women. When the Spanish colonized Mexico, men's clothing styles were affected more dramatically than those of women. In pre-Columbian times, men wore little more than a loincloth.

The loincloth is now represented by an embroidered belt or sash that many men wear around their waists.

While the palaces and pyramids of the Mayan civilization have mostly disappeared, weaving is one way that the Mayan people have sustained their culture. Eight hundred weavers from the Chiapas Highlands have formed a cooperative called Sna Jolobil, which means "The Weaver's House" in the Mayan language. The cooperative works to preserve and study ancient Mayan weaving techniques, including the complex brocades that have so much significance in the Mayan culture. Contemporary designs based on ancient symbols are also encouraged: Diamonds symbolize the unity of the earth and sky. wavy forms such as snakes symbolize the fertile earth, and forms with three vertical lines symbolize community. Butterflies, which represent the sun, often occupy the center of the brocade diamond.

The Kuna Indians of Panama are known for their colorful pieces of clothing called molas, an example of which is worn here by a young Kuna girl.

Folk Wear Traditions in Central America

The Kuna Indians of Panama also have maintained a rich folk art tradition in the clothing they both wear and sell to outsiders. Panama, the southernmost country in Central America, is a narrow bridge of land that connects South and Central America. The Kuna Indians live mostly on the San Blas Islands, a chain of islands off Panama's northern coast. They are best known for their colorful molas. Traditionally, molas were made in pairs to form the front and back panels of Kuna cotton blouses. The two panels were usually similar but never identical, symbolizing the common presence of both continuity and change. Now, they are often made as single pieces for decoration.

Molas are made using a process known as reverse appliqué. This process is complex, and of course, the most intricate examples are those that are most treasured. First, several layers of colorful fabric are assembled. Designs are then cut down into the cloth, which is folded under and finely sewn, exposing the various colors of cloth beneath the top. The criteria used to judge a mola's quality include the smoothness of the lines, the fineness of the stitches, the symmetry of the design, and the intricacy of the cutouts. Zigzags, curves, and tiny squares are the most complex shapes to cut. Mola designs come from many sources including everyday life, such as animals, scenes of nature, politics, medicine, even legends, dreams, and fantasies. Some art historians believe that this folk art tradition derives from the tradition of elaborate body painting.

Adapting Old Traditions to New Circumstances

The Hmong people of Southeast Asia also use the folk art of reverse appliqué to decorate their clothing and other textiles. Although the process is almost identical to that used by the Kuna Indians, the designs and patterns are unique to Hmong culture, which thrived until the 1970s in the mountains of Laos, Thailand, and Vietnam. The Hmong are especially known for their pandau, or flower cloths, which use reverse appliqué often embellished with embroidery to depict traditional symbols taken from nature, including such objects as an elephant's foot, ram's head, snail's house, and dragon's tail.

The lives of the Hmong people changed dramatically in the 1970s, which affected their folk art. As supporters of the United States during the Vietnam War, they were forced to flee the country when the United States withdrew its forces. Many settled in refugee camps in Thailand before eventually immigrating

GEORGEANN ROBINSON, OSAGE INDIAN RIBBONWORKER

Inspiration sometimes comes from unlikely sources. Georgeann Robinson proved this when she was honored by the Smithsonian Institution in 1982 for her work as an Osage Indian ribbonworker. The Osage Indians of Oklahoma were the unlikely beneficiaries of a change in ladies fashion in France after the French Revolution at the end of the 1700s. Suddenly it was no longer fashionable even to appear to be a member of the wealthy ruling class in France. One unforeseen result was that French merchants were left with stockpiles of fancy clothing and adornments. Hoping not to lose their profits, they exported as much as possible to the New World. There, the Osage Indians of Oklahoma found a use for the silk ribbons that were no longer adorning the finery of the French. They developed the art of ribbonwork, making ribbon shirts, skirts, and other items of clothing, and this eventually became an important expression of their identity. As Robinson accepted her honor at the ceremony for the National Heritage Fellows, she gave credit to the surprising origin of this folk art by saying, "I wish to thank the French Revolution."

Steve Siporin, *American Folk Masters*. New York: Harry N. Abrams, Inc., 1992, p. 143.

to the United States. Since they had no written language, their folk art became the means to preserve their identity and tell their stories. A new folk art evolved from the tradition of flower cloths to meet those needs as well. Called paj ntaub tib neeg, or story cloths, these elaborately embroidered panels depict both traditional Hmong stories and relate the tales of recent events in Hmong history. Traditionally, Hmong women used very bright colors on dark background cloth for both the flower and story cloths; however, they now use softer colors to appeal to Western tastes. This adaptation was crucial, since selling their folk art became an important source of income for the Hmong community.

Decorative Cloth in Africa

Bright colors, however, have remained a constant in the weaving of kente cloth from Ghana and Togo in West Africa. The vibrant colors and dramatic patterns that characterize this cloth have a long tradition in the folk clothing from these countries. Kente cloth is widely recognized as a symbol of African cultural heritage around the world.

As in many cultures, weaving is a task often carried out by men, who weave narrow, colorful strips of cloth. The strips are

Kente cloth, with its bold colors and elaborate patterns, is a symbol of African culture.

then assembled as festive clothing for special occasions such as weddings and other ceremonies. A kente is chosen for each occasion with much thought to its significance. The names given to kente cloth patterns stem from several sources, including proverbs, historical events, important rulers, and plants. Wearing kente cloth in Ghana is comparable to wearing an evening gown or tuxedo in Western cultures. Someone attending a family wedding, for example, might choose to wear a kente named Sika fre moqya ("money attracts blood"). Wearing this kente indicates trust that a relative is a hard worker and has the means to support a new family.

Though kente is a folk tradition long associated with important ceremonies, like much folk art, it has traveled and taken on new features wherever it alights in the world. In the past forty years, the bold and colorful kente designs have been incorporated into hats, ties, bags, and other accessories. The text written for an exhibit at the National Museum of African Art at the Smithsonian Institution entitled, "Wrapped in Pride," says that kente patterns "have developed a life of their own, appropriated as surface designs for everything from band aids and balloons to beach balls and Bible covers. Kente, for many, bridges two continents, evoking and celebrating a shared cultural heritage."[16] Kente strips are often sewn into academic gowns and displayed proudly at graduation ceremonies.

Weaving is one way that people from Ghana use folk art to adorn clothing and display pride in their heritage. Another folk art practiced by the Asante people of Ghana, Africa, is adinkra printing. This technique of decorating fabric entails carving symbols and geometric shapes into the hard skins of calabash gourds to make stamps. The stamps are then dipped in ink made from tree bark then applied to cloth in repeating patterns. At one time, the cloth was used only for clothing worn to funerals, (adinkra means "goodbye"), but it is now commonly found in everyday clothing and decorative household objects such as curtains. Like kente cloth, the symbols carved into the gourds have symbolic meaning in Ghana. They represent proverbs, historical events, human attitudes, plants, animals, or man made objects.

Concentric circles are the chief adinkra symbol and represent greatness or leadership. Another symbol, akoko nan, resembles the foot of a chicken. In the native Twi language of Ghana it refers to the behavior of hens that walk on their chicks yet do not harm them. This symbolizes the necessity for parents to both nurture and protect their children.

The Japanese Art of Dyeing Textiles

Dyeing cloth and making clothing are folk arts that have always been especially revered in Japan. In fact, according to Victor and Takako Hauge, many consider the making of textiles to be one of the purest forms of folk art. In their book *Folk Traditions in Japanese Art*, they write,

> Of all the craft traditions, folk textiles most easily qualify as 'folk art' in every sense of the term. Unlike ceramics and lacquer ware, which were made mostly by artisans, common-use textile production—spinning, weaving, and needlework—was carried on almost entirely by housewives and young girls, between farming and household chores.[17]

Many ordinary people made cloth for everyday use, but only some, of course, are considered artists. Uzan Kimura, for example, is renowned for the exquisite and detailed designs that he applies to cloth in a dyeing process known as yuzen. This paste resist process was invented during Japan's Edo period around 1700 and involves many painstaking steps. First, a base drawing is applied to the cloth with the juice from a plant. Then the entire design, except the part the artist is working on at the moment, is covered with a paste, traditionally made from sticky rice. Colors are applied carefully one at a time. The completed sections of the design in progress are covered with the paste in order to protect (or resist) as more colors are added. Finally, the cloth is washed

An artist demonstrates the delicate art of yuzen dyeing, whereby a design is painted in permanent dye on a piece of silk.

and the paste is removed, leaving a detailed design, often inspired by nature.

The yuzen technique is used on the kimono, the traditional Japanese garment. Kimura, like other folk artists skilled in this technique, draws his designs by hand with sharply pointed brushes. He says,

Both my materials and my ideas come from nature and everyday life. Sometimes I draw pine trees, sometimes peonies. I never deliberately search for design ideas. They often come to me by chance when I wake up in the morning. In fact, I get some of my best ideas while I'm still in bed. The morning hours are the most

DYES

Since ancient times, natural plants and minerals have provided the main sources of color used to dye the yarns embroidered and woven into cloth. Indigo, for example, which produces a deep, rich blue, was cultivated in the Middle East, Indonesia, India, the West Indies, and Latin America. Many of the most valuable and rare dyes, however, are by-products of insects and other animals. For example, the dried bodies of female cochineal beetles, harvested from cactus plants in Central and South America, produce a range of reds and pinks, depending on whether they are roasted, toasted, or boiled. However, the process of harvesting the color purple from a species of shellfish called Purpura patula pansa along the Pacific Coast of Mexico is unmatched. Jacqueline Herald, author of *World Crafts*, writes that the shellfish are still used by Mexican Indians today. To harvest the color, she explains,

> the Purpura patula is picked off wet rocks at low tide; the dyer squeezes and blows on the mollusk which, in distress, secretes a liquid onto the yarn held against it. Within the next three minutes, the substance turns from transparent to dull yellow, vivid green, and finally purple. The shellfish is then returned to the sea, only to be 'milked' again a month later.

Jacqueline Herald, *World Crafts*. Asheville: Lark Books, 1992. p. 130.

important, and unless I work hard in the morning I feel rather lazy all day.[18]

Kimura was honored in Japan as a Living National Treasure in 1955.

Another folk artist honored as a Living National Treasure is Keisuke Serizawa, who is considered a leader in Japan's folk art movement. Serizawa, like Kimura, works in textile dyeing, though he uses stencils to dye repeating patterns on the cloth. Like many admired folk artists, Serizawa's work appears simple, although the process actually involves many steps. In the book *The Enduring Crafts of Japan,* Masataka Ogawa says Serizawa's style,

> is never mistaken for that of other artists in the field. His design is vigorous and forthright, and his colors have a distinctly rural touch. It would be wrong, however, to speak of this as naiveté, for there is a certain sophistication about Serizawa's style that sets him apart from the anonymous folk artists whose traditions he upholds.[19]

Serizawa's stencil designs have been used to decorate both clothing and many other objects made of paper such as book covers, calendars, and even matchboxes.

These folk artists and others in Japan are part of an ancient tradition of respect and reverence for textiles and their decoration. Some believe this tradition stems from an old Japanese legend about the angry sun goddess who plunged the world into darkness by hiding in a cave. Blue and white cloth banners dancing in the breeze finally tempted the sun to emerge from its cave, bringing sunlight back to the world. This legend could explain why Japanese folk artists devote some of their most beautiful work to decorating textiles with symbols of nature's bounty. Blue is a common color in Japanese textiles.

Folk art has been part of apparel for as long as people have worn clothing. The clothing is used to stay warm, celebrate special occasions, indicate positions in society, and protect.

Clothing does not need to be decorated, of course, to fulfill its many practical functions. But the constant presence of folk art on clothing through time and place conveys a strong message. Decoration is not an afterthought. It does not take much extra time to weave cloth that is fine rather than coarse or dye colors that are rich and bold rather than ordinary. Folk artists decorate clothing and make cloth for the same reasons that other folk artists create pottery or carve beautiful wooden bowls. All folk art, including folk art that is worn, expresses the basic human need to make the objects of everyday life beautiful as well as practical.

4

Decorating Inside and Out

L iving spaces are personal. People work hard to build and maintain their homes. They spend many of their waking hours inside their homes tending to their families. When they are away from home, they look forward to returning, and at the end of the day they come home for the night. It makes sense, therefore, that people want to make the places they live as beautiful and as personal as possible. People's homes and sometimes the modes of transportation they use to earn their livelihoods communicate information about who they are and what they value. The way a home is decorated expresses both an individual's sense of self as well as the group that individual belongs to. That group may be large, such as a culture, or small, such as a family. Even the simplest dwellings, such as the cave dwellings of ancient man, have been embellished with wall paintings. As people become more economically secure, they tend to devote more time and thought to decorating the places they live and the furniture within those places. Decorative folk art can hang on a wall, embellish a wall, or be a wall. Folk art that is decorative is, perhaps, the most convincing testimony that folk art is not an extravagance. It is a basic necessity, which nourishes the spirit as much as food nourishes the body. Both are indispensable.

Painting Pictures on the Wall: Murals

Covering a surface with paint serves many purposes. Paint protects a surface from the effects of the weather. Paint helps wooden surfaces resist insects. It also changes the texture of surfaces, making them smooth or rough depending on how the paint is applied. But the primary purpose of painting is decoration. When immigrants first came to the New World from Europe, painting was one way they added individual character to their homes. The first homes were simple. Newcomers to the colonies copied familiar designs and techniques from their homelands. But as the standard of living improved, people built bigger and better houses. They could afford luxuries instead of devoting all their resources to the basic necessities. Also, they wanted others to notice and admire their improved circumstances. One way to do this was to decorate walls. Painting landscapes—scenes from nature—directly on the wall became a popular decorating trend in the early 19th century. Itinerant painters traveled from town to town offering their mural-painting services. At first, muralists tried to capture scenes outside the window exactly as they appeared. But a growing approval of personal expression and exuberance resulted in scenes that sprang from the artist's imagination as well as from nature itself. Artists painted farms and fields where fruit trees blossomed, and windmills and waterfalls dotted the landscapes of their imaginations. One advertisement for the work of well known mural painter Rufus Porter tempted those who could afford the luxury of having beautiful landscapes painted on their blank walls to stare at during the cheerless winter months. It invited "Those gentlemen who are desirous of spending the gloomy winter months amidst pleasant groves and verdant fields, are respectfully invited to apply. . .where a specimen of the work may be seen."[20] Moreover, nature had to be adapted somewhat to conform to the shapes of square rooms and the placement of furniture. Porter, writing in the journal *Scientific American,* advised his fellow painters to arrange

A HAITIAN LEGEND

Hector Hyppolite was an African-Haitian painter born in 1894. He worked as an apprentice shoemaker, a housepainter, furniture decorator, shipbuilder, and innkeeper. But after being invited to work at the new Le Centre d'Art in Haiti's capital city, Port-au-Prince, his reputation as one of Haiti's most important folk artists flourished. Like the other artists there, Hyppolite had no training as an artist. In fact, he used his fingers and chicken feathers instead of paintbrushes to paint his canvasses. Hyppolite's work and the work of other Haitian artists is interesting because,

> Their subjects were most often what they perceived in their everyday mundane existence and what they learned from their mythical religion, voodoo. Although they came from simple backgrounds, their paintings were full of passion and color. They managed to integrate what they saw felt and believed and express it with intensity of emotion and a childlike innocence. These men had no formal education, no visual training and basically developed their styles in isolation from the rest of the art world.

Source: MedaliaArt, "The Art of Haiti," http://www.medalia.net/Ahistory.html.

the trees to fill up bare space on the walls and allow room for the backs of chairs. The American Folk Art Museum in New York City displays large fragments of painted walls from early American houses that were probably painted by itinerant painters. Many of these old folk painting techniques have regained popularity and are used today.

Wall Stencils

While most artists painted murals by hand, some followed another of Porter's innovations by making paper patterns, or stencils, of ships, houses, and villages, so that these elements of the design could be easily repeated and used on walls in many different houses. This labor saving device helped make landscape murals more affordable. Porter claimed that an entire parlor could be landscaped with palaces, villages, mills, ships, and trees in less than five hours.

Stencils were used more commonly, however, to paint repeating patterns on walls, floors, and furniture. While gold-embellished stencil designs were first used to decorate churches in the Middle Ages, people adapted the technique for common home use in the 19th century. As the middle class grew and life-styles improved, people had homes and furniture they believed were worthy of decoration. Moreover, they wanted to display their newfound prosperity. In American homes, stenciling often mimicked the colors and patterns of European wallpaper, an alternative available only to the very wealthy. Itinerant painters traveled the countryside applying stenciled designs to interior walls and furniture, sometimes even stenciling floor cloths to imitate fancy carpets. In France, stencillers called domino paint-ers traveled around the towns and villages selling inexpensive sheets of playing cards and patterned papers that were pasted onto walls to look like wallpaper.

Painted Furniture

Stenciled designs were also applied to household items, tools, glass, and window shades. However, stenciling was especially popular as a way to decorate furniture. In the cities, sophisti-cated artisans with expensive materials worked hard to satisfy the public's interest in so-called "fancy" furniture, a trend that began in England in the late 18th and early 19th centuries. In these fancy workshops, craftsmen painted miniature landscapes, often embellished with gold leaf, onto the backs of chairs. Only the wealthy, however, could afford to buy them, since they cost about $3.50 each, which was a high price for a single chair at the time. Using stencils, however, was one way to bring down costs, since it was possible to employ workers who were less skilled. Lambert Hitchcock set up a three-story brick factory in Connecticut in 1825 to make chairs where many workers used inexpensive stencils to apply designs. The fruits, flowers, and leaves were then embellished and shaded by hand. Hitchcock sold his chairs for $1.50, so the less wealthy citizens could afford them.

However, the work of country artisans best expresses the spirit of folk art. They used the same graining techniques on furniture that city painters used to make simple pine doors and fireplace mantels appear to be rich mahogany and walnut. In fact, almost all furniture built in the country was painted to disguise its patchwork construction from woods of many kinds and colors. Paint also protected the furniture from insects. Country furniture makers became quite skilled at producing wood finishes that looked like cedar, rosewood, curly and bird's eye maple, birch, walnut, and mahogany. Sometimes, they simulated even more exotic materials, such as tortoise shells. Rebecca Sawyer-Fay writes that as they searched from town to town for commissions,

> country painters learned to take advantage of the least expensive, most readily available materials on hand. Paint recipes made use of pigments formulated from soot and lampblack, clay, bark, leaves, berries, and animal blood; these were bound with skim and butter milk. Artisans cut stencils from leather, paper, and linen, and found that the long fur of a squirrel's tail could be made into serviceable brushes.[21]

Stenciled and freehand designs also decorated beds, cupboards, chairs, chests, tables, and boxes. The designs were often symbolic. For example, a tulip with three petals represented the Holy Trinity. A lion stood for courage, and a peacock was a religious symbol for the Resurrection.

Painting Roses

Painting designs on furniture was not limited to the United States of course. The creative urge to embellish the walls and furnishings flourished throughout the world. Decorative painting has a long history in Norway, for example. Norwegian rosemaling is a folk art that has decorated walls and furniture as well as drinking vessels there since the 18th century. Rosemaling literally means rose painting, and indeed, that flower remains a common subject for these decorations, which are composed of three basic brushstrokes: a C, a S, and a circle. The acanthus leaf is another favorite motif. This image may have originated in Norway with the Vikings, who had been impressed with the

Painted tin, or toleware, was popular in the United States in the 19th century.

acanthus leaves that wrapped around the Corinthian columns in ancient Greece. Some of Norway's most accomplished folk artists brought the art of rosemaling with them to the midwest region of the United States in the mid-1800s, where the tradition still thrives today.

Painted tin, or toleware, is another decorative art that originated in the Far East, spread to Europe, and settled in America, where it reached the height of its popularity in the 19th century. Toleware is sometimes called japanware, since the pigments used in the best toleware came from Japan. Toleware was inexpensive and readily available. Tin pieces were first painted with asphaltum, a black or dark brown base coat made from coal. When dried, this coating became hard and shiny. Then lively designs of flowers, leaves, and swirls of paint in bright primary colors and orange were added.

Portraits and Other Framed Paintings

Paintings that hang on the wall are another way that people in many countries, including the United States, decorate their homes. Before photography became widespread in the mid 1800s, people relied on artists' portraits to depict their faces, their families, and their possessions. In the United States, folk art painters called limners traveled the countryside painting portraits and scenes from everyday life. These folk artists had often begun their careers painting signs and the outside of houses and were unschooled in fine art techniques such as shadowing and perspective. Their work, therefore, usually appears flat. Their technique, often called primitive, was not necessarily intended to portray accurate likenesses of their subjects. Mary Emmerling, an author of several books about folk art, explains that in the late 18th and early 19th centuries,

> Scores of anonymous artists would prepare costumed bodies on canvas during winter months, and in the

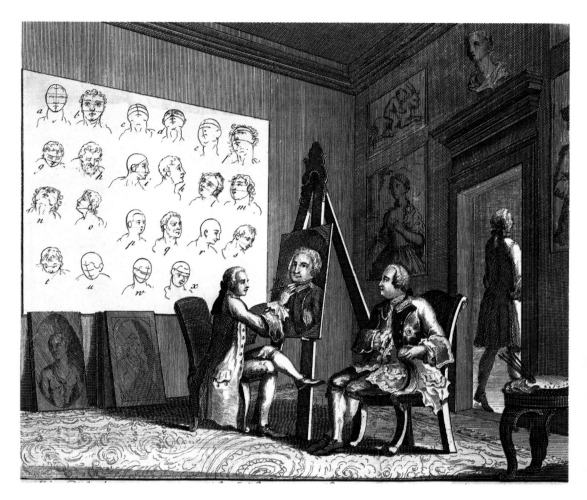

spring set out with their stock to hunt for customers. Patrons would then choose appropriate finery from a painter's inventory, and the painter would provide a relatively realistic head for a decoratively dressed torso.[22]

Sometimes, people would order a portrait by mail, sending a list of the objects to include in the painting, such as jewelry or fine furniture, to indicate their social standing. Beautiful landscapes visible through windows behind the figure suggested land ownership. Books indicated education. These folk paintings often provide the best information available about attitudes, fashions, and important events of the time. Once photography became

Before the invention of photography, many people relied on limners, or untrained folk artists, to paint portraits of themselves or of their families.

widespread, most of the folk painters lost their businesses. Some decided to change their occupations, replacing their brushes and canvasses with cameras.

Decorative Wood Carving

Woodcarving is another decorating technique with a rich folk history, especially in heavily forested areas where wood is plentiful. Mountainous communities in Europe, such as areas of Switzerland and Germany that were isolated before the advent of modern communication and transportation, developed distinctive styles. In Norway, for example, intricate borders of intertwined vines were often carved onto the outside surfaces of farmhouses. Trond Gjerdi writes that Norwegian folk art was

> created mainly by small freehold and tenant farmers working in their spare time. We find, too, itinerant craftsmen going from farm to farm, carrying out orders for individual patrons. The majority of the so-called folk artists were people forced to seek extra work in order to supplement their meager incomes.[23]

Norwegian woodcarvers often carved elaborate dragon heads, which were then placed at the highest peaks of the rooftops. According to legend, the heads protected the human inhabitants from evil spirits. The acanthus plant, a popular image in Norwegian rose painting, was also a favorite theme of Norwegian woodcarvers. It was first used to decorate a church altarpiece in the 1600s, but its popularity quickly spread, and craftsmen carved acanthus to decorate the interior of homes as well as cupboards and clock cabinets. Over time, woodcarvers in Norway used their carving skills to decorate smaller household objects such as butter molds and cheese boxes.

Woodcarvers in Micronesia, Melanesia, and Polynesia (groups of islands in the South Pacific) have very different purposes for carving wood. In these parts of the world, which include Hawaii, Tahiti, and New Zealand, the center of the community's life is the sea. Moreover, dependence on the sea

has created rich folk traditions. The finest woodcarvers in the Eastern Solomon Islands build and decorate wooden canoes used to fish. When islanders spot flocks of seabirds, they believe that the gods are happy, and the time is right to set out in their canoes to fish. The best woodcarvers in the Trobriand Islands, off the coast of New Guinea, practice their woodcarving skills by carving canoes for trading voyages. Their most important work is making lagim, the decorative splashboards for the prow (the front) and stern (the back) of the canoes. The spiraling lagim have two wings like those of a butterfly, though they are not symmetrical, since the outrigger style of these canoes results in more sea spray from one side. Images of snakes, birds, fish, and snails are worked into the designs, and each carver's style is unique. Another decorated feature of these trading canoes is the tabuya, a board that fits at a perpendicular angle to the lagim. Frequently, an image of a white heron is worked into the tabuya's

Woodcarvers in Papua New Guinea adorn their canoes with decorative carvings, such as this white bird, to bring good luck to those on the voyage.

design, since Trobriand Islanders believe the graceful heron is a bird of perfect balance and will bring good luck to the voyage.

Woodcarving, like many folk arts, traveled to the shores of the New World with European settlers. The Germans who settled in Pennsylvania, New England, and North Carolina were among the immigrant groups who had the most impact on the development of folk art in the New World. These Pennsylvania Germans, as they were known, continued to make furniture and build houses in the styles they carried from their homelands. One of the most famous Pennsylvania German woodcarvers was Wilhelm Schimmel, who made his living by traveling from town to town selling and trading his woodcarvings of birds. Schimmel is most famous for his carvings of eagles, which he then covered with a white paste called gesso and then brightly painted.

Using Resin in Japan and Colombia

Another technique used to decorate wooden objects that has a long folk history is the art of lacquer ware. In Japan, the art of decorating with lacquer was perfected hundreds of years ago and is still practiced by some of Japan's leading folk artists. Lacquer is a shiny coat of resin that is painted over wood and produces a hard finish, which is then decorated in various ways. One technique known as "maki-e" entails sprinkling gold or silver dust on the wet lacquer to produce a design. Another technique called "chushitsu" is reminiscent of the molas of the Kuna Indians and pa ndau of the Hmong. Like the layers of colored cloth used to produce those textiles, chushitsu involves layering colored lacquers, then carving a design into the lacquer, which reveals the various colors beneath the surface. Sometimes, a design is engraved into a single-colored lacquered surface, and colors are then inlaid. Lacquer designs are most often applied to wooden trays, utensils, and boxes. Gonroku Matsuda (1896–1986) was a lacquer artist who was named one of Japan's Living National

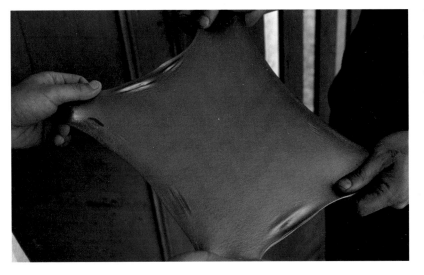

Two Colombian artists prepare barniz by stretching dyed resin into a paper-thin sheet.

Treasures in 1955. Sometimes called the "Mozart of Maki-e" because, like the musician, he learned his art as a very young child, he is especially renowned for his work in the art of maki-e in which gold dust is applied to wet lacquer. The work is painstaking and finely detailed. Of the amount of time he spends on his art, Matsuda says, "If you worry about the time you will never produce a decent piece of lacquer."[24] Matsuda's work ranged from small food bowls to large pieces, such as screens used for interior decorating. Many other lacquer artists in Japan continue these folk traditions to decorate wooden objects found in the home.

Wooden objects in Colombia in South America are decorated with another technique involving resin. In this case, the resin is obtained from the seedpods of a tree that grows at high altitudes only in Colombia. Originally, the purpose of the resin coating was to make wooden objects watertight, but now barnizwork is considered purely decorative. The Spanish coined the word "barniz" when they colonized South America, most likely confusing it with the European term for varnish, which is also a hard, moisture-resistant finish.

Barniz artisans heat and hammer the seed pods to separate them from the resin, then dye the resin and stretch it by hand to create a paper-thin sheet. Designs are cut freehand from this sheet of resin and applied to wooden objects, using the warmth of the hand to soften them. Intricate designs of many colors can take days to complete, since each area of color must be applied individually. The most common motifs are paisaje, or landscapes, as well as floral and abstract designs. The piece is then sealed with a protective coat of clear lacquer.

Decorating the Means of Transportation

Tap-Tap trucks are a common sight in Haiti. Their vivid artwork, often religious in nature, is representative of Haitian culture.

One purpose of decoration is to personalize things that are otherwise impersonal. While decorated objects accomplish those goals in a small way, decorating the structures that people live in and the vehicles that move them from one place to another is more conspicuous. Graffiti, a type of decoration, on freight

A gypsy caravan, with its bright colors and elaborate decorations, is a moveable work of folk art.

trains, for example, attracts attention across the country. Folk art of this sort is still highly visible in Haiti, one of the world's poorest countries, where brightly painted buses called Tap-Tap trucks ferry passengers around the country. Tap-Taps are often painted with flowers and religious slogans.

In England, folk art of this type is seen on narrow boats, so-named because they navigate the narrow canals that criss-cross the country. In the 19th century these barely seven-foot wide wooden boats often housed entire families. Their painted scenes of roses and castles were visible to all as they moved along the canals, pulled by horses walking on a footpath next to the canal. Painted narrow boats still exist on England's canals.

The Gypsy caravan is another vehicle that was decorated in the folk art style. The name "Gypsy" itself is thought to be a shortened form of "Egyptian," as many Gypsies trace their earliest ancestors to Egypt. Gypsies were mostly nomadic. They moved from place to place in Europe and the United Kingdom, carrying their belongings in elaborately painted horse-drawn wagons, or caravans. Designs sometimes hinted at the ethnic origin of each family. A family with roots in India, for example, might paint images of the Himalayan Mountains on the sides of its caravan.

Decorative folk art serves many purposes and encompasses many techniques. It does not change the function of an object, a home, or a vehicle. Yet, its universal presence testifies to its importance. The way people decorate expresses ideas about their lifestyle, personality, and worldview. Wherever people establish roots, they decorate to communicate who they are, where they are from, and what they want others to know about them.

5

Celebration and Ritual

One type of folk art that is especially vibrant and expressive is the art that accompanies celebrations and rituals around the world. When people celebrate, they set aside their ordinary lives momentarily to focus fully on the event at hand. Preparing for the event and participating in the event entail traditions that connect people to their families and their cultures. Most people believe that those connections give life its most important meaning. Appreciating the folk art associated with a culture's celebrations and rituals helps people understand that culture in the deepest way possible.

Paper Streamers and Paper Cranes

In Japan, folk arts that use paper are featured during many important occasions. One popular folk art is paper folding, or origami, which is used for recreation and to celebrate births, weddings, and funerals. Origami, originally a Chinese folk art, was popularized in Japan in the 1700s after publication of the book *How to Fold 1000 Cranes*, which elevated the origami crane

The annual Tanabata, or Star Festival, in Japan is marked by thousands of colorful paper streamers hanging from almost everywhere.

to a place of honor. The crane, a popular image in Japanese art, is treasured for its strength and grace, and because it chooses its partner for life. Anyone who folds one thousand cranes, according to Japanese custom, will receive his or her greatest wish. Couples who are about to marry fold one thousand cranes to decorate their wedding festivities in an ancient custom called sembazuru. This task, which takes time and patience, symbolizes the couple's intention to spend the rest of their lives together living in harmony. Folk customs also connect certain traits with various paper colors. Red, for instance, represents strong love and passion. Orange is associated with enthusiasm, while yellow symbolizes freedom and joy.

Paper also figures prominently in the Japanese Tanabata or Star Festival, celebrated on July 7 each year, when folk art decorations festoon the streets of Japan's towns and villages. All over Japan, red, yellow, green, white, and black paper streamers hang

A favorite true Japanese story is one about a little girl named Sadako and one thousand cranes. Sadako was two years old when the atomic bomb was dropped on Hiroshima. This is the story of how she and the origami crane became a symbol of peace that is recognized worldwide:

A young Japanese girl named Sadako Sasaki was born in 1943. As she grew up, Sadako was a strong, courageous and athletic girl. In 1955, at age 11, Sadako was diagnosed with leukemia, the 'atom bomb disease.' Her best friend told her of an old Japanese legend, which said that anyone who folds a thousand paper cranes would be granted a wish. Sadako wished to get well again. She started to work on the paper cranes and completed over 1000 before dying on October 25, 1955, at the age of 12. Although her wish was not granted, she never gave up. In 1958, a statue of Sadako holding a golden crane was unveiled in Hiroshima Peace Park. Children all over Japan, who were inspired by Sadako's courage, helped to collect money for the project. Their wish is inscribed at the bottom of the statue. It reads: 'This is our cry; this is our prayer; peace in the world.'

Today people all over the world fold paper cranes and send them to Sadako's monument in Hiroshima.

"The Sadako Story," http://www.sadako.org/sadakostory.htm.

Japanese legend says that anyone who folds a thousand paper cranes will be granted a wish.

from bamboo branches, rippling in the breeze. Handwritten wishes for success, wealth, love, and health, or love poems are written on the streamers in towns and cities all over Japan.

The streamers symbolize the weaving of threads, an important part of the Tanabata story retold each year. According to that story, a weaver princess named Orihime and a cow herder prince named Hikoboshi, lived and played together in space. The king became angry at their constant togetherness and banished them to opposite sides of the galaxy. They were allowed to meet only on the seventh day of the seventh month each year. Other brightly colored paper Tanabata decorations represent casting nets, which symbolize the hope for a good year of fishing or farming. Colorful paper bags symbolize the wish for abundance. In Okinawa, an island off the coast of Japan, people light lanterns and float candles and bamboo leaves down rivers and streams. The flames symbolize the stars, while the rivers stand for the separation of Orihime and Hikoboshi. It is considered bad luck if it rains on the night of the Tanabata Festival, since the prince and princess must then wait a full year before they can meet again.

In Puerto Rico, mask-making is an ancient folk art that is still practiced today. Pictured is a traditional vejigante mask.

Scary Masks of Puerto Rico

Folk art that expresses a different mood is prominent at carnivals in the country of Puerto Rico. Puerto Rico has a diverse culture that is a combination of native Taino Indians, and descendants of both Spanish settlers and African slaves. One tradition that combines aspects of all these cultures is mask making. Making masks is an old Puerto Rican folk art

PUERTO RICAN MASK MAKER

Fernando Luis Perez Lopez began making masks when he was only 8 years old. Today, his creations are admired and exhibited throughout Puerto Rico and sell for several hundred dollars each. Like many of the best folk artists, Perez's creations are grounded in tradition and then enhanced with his own creative spirit. He explains, "No se puede limitar su imaginacion artistica cuando no tiene limites [You cannot limit imagination since it has no limits]." Perez is particularly proud of his first major solo exhibition in 1999 at the Centro Ceremonial Indigena de Tibes in his native town of Ponce, Puerto Rico. The exhibition, titled "Evolution," established Perez as a premier mask artist in Puerto Rico.

El Coqui Galleries, "Vejigantes Masks," http://www.elcoquigifts.com/specialvejigante.asp.

that has undergone a dramatic revival in recent years. These masks, called caretas, are made of paper-mache and appear part human and part animal. Every mask sports menacing horns, scary expressions, and bulging eyes. Simple masks may have two or three horns, while the most elaborate sometimes have hundreds. At one time, the colors of the masks were limited to black, red, and yellow, the colors of fire, but modern masks are sometimes blue and white or pastel. The tradition of caretas stems from the practice in medieval Spain in which parades of strict religious believers wore masks depicting the devil to scare people whose beliefs did not conform to strict church doctrine. That custom combined with a tribal African custom of wearing masks to ward off evil spirits has resulted in the caretas worn today. The Taino people are also believed to have been skilled mask-makers. The masked carnival-goers, called vejigantes, roam the streets during the carnivals, sending children running in fear. They represent the devil in the battle between good and evil.

Circles and Lines: the Original Peoples of Australia

In Australia, the folk art that is part of the ceremonies and rituals of the aboriginal people dates back many thousands of years before Europeans landed on the continent's shores. Only the name "aborigine" has European origins, since Europeans gave that name to the people they found living in there in the 1700s. It comes from the Latin term "ab origine," which means "from the beginning." However, different groups have different names, according to where they live and the language they speak. One folk art found in many parts of Australia is the making and carving of churingas, oval wood or stone slabs used in the ceremony that initiates young boys into adulthood. Churingas vary greatly in size. The smallest can be merely one inch long, while large churingas, called dancing boards, can be up to seventeen feet from one end to the other. The symbols painted on the churingas help tell the legends and stories that explain the totems or symbols that represent each aboriginal group. Totems can relate to plants, animals, or inanimate objects. The symbols painted on churingas usually include some combination of circles, lines, dots, zigzags, and other geometric shapes. Roman Black, an artist who wrote a book about aboriginal art explains that the meanings of the symbols can vary. He writes,

> The most frequently used patterns of concentric circles may represent a water-hole, fruit, a tree, a grass-seed cake, a locality, a rat's nest, or the body of a spider. Another typical symbol, the U-shaped curve, may represent a resting place or men sitting down.[25]

When a string is tied through a hole in one end of the churinga and it is whirled overhead, it produces a low humming sound that is believed to be the voice of a dangerous spirit. These whirled churingas are known as "bullroarers." The churinga is a sacred object taken out only during the initiation ceremony.

The Tiwi people who live on Melville and Bathhurst Islands off the northern coast of Australia use two forms of folk art for the pukumani, or funeral ceremony, which takes place six months after a person has died. Family and friends paint their bodies with the same patterns that are applied to the wooden funeral or pukumani poles that are carved by relatives before the ceremony. The pukumani poles can reach more than twenty feet high and vary from simple cylinders to elaborately carved structures resembling human figures. The dead person's family totem, or symbol, may also be part of the pole's decoration. Red, yellow, and white bands of color, vertical or wavy lines, circles, and ovals painted on their bodies are believed to prevent those who attend the funeral from being taken to the spirit world along with their deceased friend or relative. The pukumani ceremony is public and combines song, dance, and sculpture to tell the story and celebrate the life of the person who has died. At the end of the funeral ceremony the poles are fitted into holes dug around the gravesite, where they remain until the paint wears away and the wood deteriorates. Small bags, called yimwalini, made of bark are also decorated to match the designs on the decorated poles and painted bodies. They are then presented as gifts to the friends and family who dance at the funeral. These customs continue today on these islands.

Totems of the Northwest Coast

Totem poles are also an important part of the folk art and ritual of several Native American groups of the coastal Pacific Northwest. The first totem poles were carved from mature red cedar trees and carried to potlatch ceremonies. These large gatherings of many clans were occasions for the exchange of food, stories, and gifts between families. The Chinook word "potlatch," means "giving." Totem poles identified each family group. Meanings were assigned to the various fish, animals, birds, and

Totem poles are an important part of Northwest Native American folk art. Each symbol carved into a totem pole has meaning, and is used to communicate a story.

other designs that helped each family tell its story and interpret certain experiences. The Manataka American Indian Council, a non-profit group based in Arkansas that is devoted to preserving Native American customs, says:

> Totem figures are not gods. Totems are not worshiped like religious icons nor used as a talisman. They were never used to ward off evil spirits. A totem pole may be compared to the symbols in the Great Seal of the United States or a coat of arms. These national emblems are roughly equivalent to the meaning bound up in a totem pole, except they identified clans instead of an entire nation.[26]

The meanings of some symbols were secret, known only to a tribe's elders. Others were commonly understood. The eagle, for

*A*griculture is the primary means of survival for the Otomi Indians, who live in the east-central Mexican plateau of Sierra de Puebla. They have a long folk history of using cutout paper figures to ensure good crops, bring success in love, and ward off illness. Many of their religious practices center on the spirits they believe to be embodied by seeds, the crops they grow, the animals they raise, the rain, sun, and other natural forces. The intricate amate cutouts are used in religious rituals to represent those spirits. The amate paper is made from the bark of the fig and mulberry trees in a process developed by the Mayan Indians. The paper is folded in half and cut with knives or scissors to create figures with perfect symmetry. The paper cutouts are also used by the Otomi to teach their children about their cultural heritage.

instance, represents great strength and leadership. An eagle on a family's totem pole indicates prestige in the community. The presence of a killer whale on a family's totem is a protector and a symbol of good. A hawk with its keen eyesight is a symbol of strength. Totem poles are still carved in the Pacific Northwest today and continue to represent the pride and traditions of the Northwest Native American peoples.

The Spirit of the Southwest

The carving of kachina dolls is a folk art that is popular among the Hopi Indians in the Southwest. The Hopi believe that everything that exists in the world—even death and the sun's energy—has two forms: the visible object itself and its spirit. Kachinas represent the spirits of all things, such as plants and animals, wild food, birds, insects, and even the power of a neighboring tribe. But because spirits are invisible, the Hopi need a concrete way to interact with them. In order to do that, dancers wear costumes representing kachina spirits and perform ritual dances. The dancers also carve replicas of their kachina costumes and present them to the children. These replicas, called tihu by the Hopi and kachina dolls to others, are not considered toys. They are believed to embody a small part of the spirit they represent and so are carefully displayed in Hopi households. The kachina dolls teach the children about the Kachina spirits and help them to learn the Hopi stories.

The art of making kachina dolls has changed dramatically since the first ones were carved hundreds of years ago before the Spanish invasion of North America. At one time, all kachina dolls were carved from the roots of cottonwood trees found near rivers in the southwest. However, as people began collecting kachina dolls and more of them were produced, the supply of cottonwood roots diminished. Other kinds of wood are now used, though kachina dolls made from cottonwood roots are still

Native American Kachina dolls are not toys. They represent the spirits of all things, and each doll is thought to embody a small part of the particular spirit it represents.

highly prized. The tools used to make them have also changed. Carvers now use steel tools in place of the stone tools that were used long ago. However, the paint and details of kachina doll costumes have changed most dramatically. While natural materials, such as iron oxide, copper ore, and colored clays, were used originally to make the paints that covered the bodies and costumes, acrylic paints are now more common. The materials used to make the costumes have been most affected by modern laws governing the protection of native species of plants and animals. While religion once determined the specific feathers used on each kachina doll, for example, the Department of Fish and Game now closely monitors and regulates the feathers used on kachina dolls. Chicken, sparrow, and artificial feathers now replace eagle, red-tailed hawk, and prairie falcon.

There have been other changes, too. In the 1960s, for instance, gigantic, life size kachina dolls became popular. Miniature kachina dolls that conserved both space and materials soon replaced these. Carvers added moveable joints to their repertoire in the 1970s to mimic the movements of kachina dancers. People who collect kachina dolls are faced with an ever-changing array of possibilities. Barton Wright in his book, *Hopi Kachinas* notes that it is impossible to collect every kachina doll style because,

> Kachina dolls are an art form that is constantly changing. It is an art practiced by many artisans who live in twelve different reservation villages as well as neighboring towns. The dolls they produce are carved and painted within their conception of the kachina type. Some carvers have excellent memories and others do not, even though they are striving in virtually every instance to produce an accurate kachina image.[27]

Hopi do not worship kachinas. They treat them as partners who are interested in their welfare. Since kachinas are spirits, no one can actually see them, but the Hopi view certain natural events as proof that kachinas exist. Wright says that "Their existence is inferred from the steam which rises from food and whose loss does not change the form of the food, the mist rising from a spring on a cold morning, or the cloud which forms above a mountain top."[28] The Hopi believe that when rain clouds appear over the mountains, those clouds represent the spirits of the rain-bringing kachinas, who bring much-needed rain to the people and hide the faces of other kachinas. The tradition of carving kachina dolls remains an active and dynamic folk art.

The Zuni Indians, another tribe from the Southwest, also carve figures, called fetishes, that have spiritual significance. These small figures, which can depict birds, animals, or humans, are usually carved from semi-precious stones such as turquoise, lapis, and marble. An artist considers the color and characteristics of each stone before deciding which fetish to carve. Some

The Zuni Indians carve figures, called fetishes, from semi-precious stones. Pictured here is a Zuni fetish necklace of animals, birds, and fish.

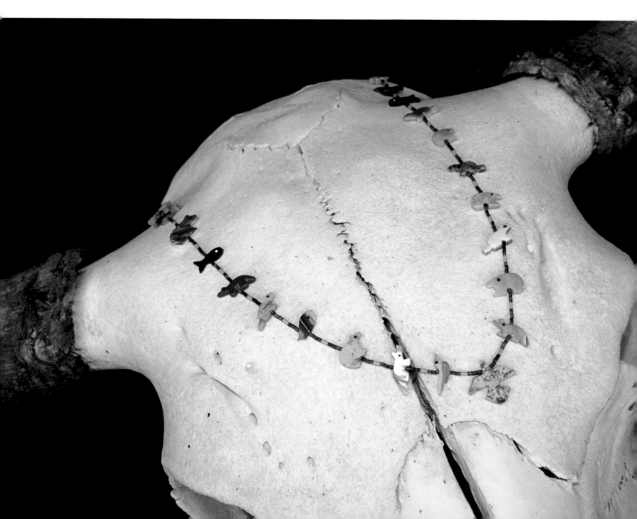

fetishes are carved from other materials, such as shell, antler, or wood. Tiny pieces of coral and silver are sometimes inlaid to enhance the design and increase the value of the fetish.

The Zuni believe that a fetish actually embodies the spirit of the figure it portrays and that it possesses magic powers. Its purpose is to heal and protect both the fetish carver and the person who buys the fetish and takes care of it. In fact, some Zuni believe that the amount of good luck that a fetish brings is directly related to the amount of loving care it receives. To that end, Zuni feed their fetishes by placing them occasionally in a dish of cornmeal. Moreover, small offerings often accompany a fetish when it is purchased. Tiny arrowheads, feathers, and stones are sometimes connected to the fetish by a leather string. The first Zuni fetishes were hunting fetishes that were taken on the hunt to ensure success. The Zuni also believe that one fetish guards each cardinal direction: the mountain lion guards the north, the badger guards the south, the bear guards the west, and the wolf guards the east. In addition, the mole guards the inner earth, and the eagle guards the sky. Each animal also embodies various traits and characteristics. The bear, for example, embodies strength in addition to protecting the west. The turtle is the earthly incarnation of long life, and the horse is believed to possess innate healing powers.

And in Return, I Promise . . .

Grateful Brazilians who have been cured of various ailments place doll-size versions of heads, legs, arms, and other body parts on altars to give thanks for relief from their afflictions. These offerings, called milagres in Portugese, or "ex-votos," can be seen at hundreds of shrines throughout the country. One of the most famous shrines is Sao Francisco das Chagas in northeastern Brazil, where tens of thousands of ex-votos are offered each year. An ex-voto of the hand, for example, attests to the cure of an infection or broken bone. A tiny misshapen leg shows thanks for the healing of a twisted ankle. At the American Folk Art Museum in New York City, a small detailed head and neck

Folk artists carved these ex-votos of newborns perhaps as thanks for the safe birth of a child.

ex-voto depicts a tiny mustached face that droops on one side, perhaps evidence of a stroke.

Folk artists in Brazil craft ex-votos in all sizes from many materials, though most are carved of wood. Moreover, the craftsmanship, like all folk art, varies widely. Some ex-votos may show fine details such as the lines in the palm of a hand or tiny toenails on a foot. Others are abstract, merely suggesting the forms of body parts and torsos. The influence of African sculpture is evident in many of these ritual objects, since African traditions play a large role in the culture of Brazil. Some pilgrims who journey to a shrine to give thanks are more concerned with their cure than the quality of the ex-voto they place on the altar. Marion Oettinger, Jr., explains that

> At the rural shrine devoted to Sao Severino, *milagres* are rented to pilgrims as they enter the church. 'I'll take an arm. Give me a leg, please.' Devotees then line up to place their ex-votos on the altar. A few minutes later, a small sliding door opens next to the altar, and a hand appears to gather up the accumulated pile of objects for recycling. Rental income is divided between the church and the owners of the land on which the shrine is located.[29]

Transportation ex-votos such as tiny replicas of cars, buses, airplanes, and trains are also common. They testify to the wish for a safe journey in a land of hazardous roads and remote countryside.

The custom of offering ex-votos in Brazil is part of a larger tradition common in many Latin American countries: one that expresses an agreement between those who believe in higher powers and the powers themselves. The agreement is based on a promise that if someone prays for a favor and the favor is granted, the grateful recipient will return the favor in some way. Making a long journey to a particular shrine and placing an ex-voto on the altar of that shrine is one way of returning the favor. The origins of most rituals, including the placing of ex-votos on shrines, are so longstanding they are hard to trace, but the folk art associated with all of those rituals undergoes changes as available resources, populations, communities, and needs change. Those changes may be subtle, or they may be dramatic. But they are inevitable.

6

Dolls, Carousels, and Other Amusements

Play is the work of children, and toys are the tools of this important work. Children all over the world play with toys that are very similar to one another. Sometimes the only difference between the toys in one country and another is the material used to make them. John Darcy Noble, a past curator of Dolls and Toys at the Museum of the City of New York, writes that "In reviewing the playthings of our past in conjunction with those of other cultures, one is struck by the similarities, by the expressions of the urge to play that are common to all mankind."[30] Dolls, pull toys, wind-powered, toys, wind-up, and toys that are powered only by the imagination are all important to the children. And the toys that children play with, like the houses people live in and the foods they eat, reveal attitudes and customs that can be missing from written accounts. And indeed, they are often the best clues available to solve history's mysteries.

Simple Dolls from the Colonies

The doll in its many forms is perhaps the most universal childhood toy. Children have always played with dolls. Dolls have

been unearthed from ancient Egyptian tombs and prehistoric Arctic villages. Even though the Puritans frowned on child's play, their moral teachings were not enough to stem their children's natural impulse to play. Wendy Lavitt explains that in spite of stern warnings, Puritan children created their dolls. She says,

> somehow dolls were born, in clandestine moments from utilitarian objects. These dolls, fashioned with more love than expense, became part of American folk art. While made from whatever scraps were at hand, they possessed a unique beauty that shone through their simple appearance.[31]

Cloth dolls were, quite simply, a childhood necessity. They took many forms and were constructed of many materials, from the simplest stuffed rag to elaborate creations that were embroidered and embellished with fur. Most cloth dolls in the early days of

Throughout history, the doll has been a treasured childhood toy. Pictured here are traditional Mexican dolls.

this country, however, were made of linen or unbleached cotton and stuffed with sawdust, bran, or straw. Sometimes the dolls' cloth faces were replaced many times as the originals wore out from heavy play. Hair was often yarn or thread—whatever was available in the sewing basket. Sometimes animal hair and even human hair were used.

A folk doll belonging to a slave child from the 1830s.

Dolls from the South Before and After the Civil War

Dolls from the South are a powerful example of how history can be interpreted by "reading" its artifacts, especially its folk art. Most dolls were made to amuse children and not to prove anything. In the American South before the Civil War, folk dolls made by loving parents or the slaves that cared for the children provide many clues to the attitudes in the South about slavery. They also help to explain the complicated nature of the relationships between the children of the plantation owners and the slaves who cared for them. These women, known as mammies, were slaves, and they were also mothers, who lavished love and attention on both their own children and the children in their care. Wendy Lavitt notes that

> In the plantation nursery, the mammy reigned. To help in raising both the master's children and her own, she conjured up a variety of amusements, including

dolls she made in her own image. Some of these dolls cradled black or white infants in their arms. The mammies themselves, made from cloth, nuts, or even rubber nipples from baby bottles, always wore the traditional bandanna scarf wrapped tight around the head.[32]

After the Civil War, African American dolls reflected the changed social circumstances of many African Americans. These dolls were now dressed as teachers and fashionable ladies. Many African American women used the sewing skills learned as slaves to become dressmakers, which gave them access to scraps of fine silks and velvets to sew the finery for their children's new dolls. Some dolls after the Civil War also depicted racial stereotypes, revealing the mixed emotions about the War's outcome. Yet, like other artifacts, the dolls themselves bear no judgments. They do, however, help trace the experience of African Americans.

Dolls that Smile and Dolls that Frown

Children of the Arctic region played with dolls made of bone, antler, stone, ivory, animal skins, and cloth. The dolls relay the stories of how people survived in this harsh climate. Every member of a closely-knit family had an important role, with different dolls representing each role. Boy dolls with kayaks and harpoons and girl dolls with tiny doll-babies snugly cuddled within thick skin parkas leave no question about who performed each task. Greasy rag dolls tell of make-believe whale blubber parties, the Arctic equivalent of the modern doll's tea party. If a doll's accessories are not sufficient to determine its gender, the turn of its mouth leaves no question. Boy dolls' mouths turn up in happy smiles, while the mouths of girl dolls turn down in permanent frowns.

The topsy-turvy is a folk doll that is unique to America. These dolls were constructed with two heads, one on either end, and the body concealed by a long skirt. They were sometimes used as props to tell favorite stories such as *Little Red Riding Hood*. In that case, the head on one end might portray Little Red Riding Hood, while the head on the opposite end revealed either the grandmother or the scary wolf. Topsy-turvy dolls played a different role in the South before the Civil War. During that period, they were frequently constructed with one white and one black head. Some folk historians believe these dolls provided a means for young slave children to own a coveted, but forbidden white doll, which they could quickly flip to the other side if the plantation's overseer suddenly appeared.

Dolls Made by the Woodland Indians

The Native Americans who lived in the forests of the East and Midwest United States depended on corn as their primary source of food. As a result, children of the Iroquois, Oneida, and Penobscot tribes played with dolls made from corncobs and cornhusks. Some dolls modeled cornhusk clothing on bodies made of wood, apples, rawhide, and cloth or combinations of these materials. Women of the Osage, Micmac, Sauk, Fox, and other Great Lakes tribes learned to cut and sew complicated geometric patterns from bright ribbons obtained in trade with white settlers. This ribbon work became part of their own clothing, and the leftovers helped dress the fancy dolls made for the children and to sell to traders. Floral beadwork adorned the buckskin and rag dolls made by Chippewa Native American parents from North Dakota and Minnesota for their children.

The Seminole Native Americans dressed their carved wood or palmetto fiber dolls in colorful cotton patchwork clothing, a technique learned from their white Southern neighbors. Strands of fine beads circled the dolls' necks, reflecting the style of Seminole women, who began collecting strands of beads when they were small children.

Fancy Dolls with Fancy Beads

Studying the changes in Native American doll clothing helps to understand how the cultures of the settlers were incorporated by the Native Americans they eventually displaced. The Plains tribes, for example, depended on buffalo and deer meat for survival, and it follows that their dolls were made primarily from animal skins. Early doll clothing from the Plains was fairly simple and unadorned, but after white traders introduced beads to the Sioux and Comanche, intricate beadwork became a popular way to decorate all clothing, including the clothing on the dolls. Wendy Lavitt explains that beadwork was important to the Plains tribes. She writes, "Learning the complex beadwork patterns was an important part of an Indian girl's childhood. While pioneer children embroidered samplers and stitched patchwork quilts, Plains Indian girls practiced beadwork on their dolls' clothing."[33] Many of the most elaborate dolls, however, were displayed inside the teepee. The children played only with the simple rag dolls that could be dragged around and subjected to rain, dirt, and the loving abuse of outside play without being ruined.

Soon after white traders introduced beads to Native Americans, their once simple dolls began to be adorned with intricate beadwork.

Northwest Coast Native American Dolls

Dolls of the Northwest coast also endured rough treatment, partly from play and partly from the fog and damp that pervades these rain-drenched regions. Oregon's Yurok Native American dolls are distinguished by the blue tint of the clay used to form their bodies, while the Klamath in Southern Oregon made dolls from a variety of materials including wood, shredded bark, long grasses, and clay. Further north, Klikitat Native American parents fashioned their children's dolls from steamed leather and dressed them in parka trimmed with fur. Noses were added later, and eyes and mouths were often shaped with beads. The Tlingit Native Americans made simple dolls from pebbles, using rocks to pound them into their finished shapes. Although the Northwest Coast Indian groups are renowned for their wood-carving, this skill was devoted mostly to carving totem poles, canoes, masks, and other ceremonial objects. Like children everywhere, Northwest Coast Native American children often played with the simplest rag dolls.

Doll making is an expression of cultural values and traditions. Just as Barbie dolls help to decode certain modern American values, dolls from any culture help to explain that culture's distinctive styles and values. The "art" of a folk art doll might be as simple as a quirky smile embroidered on a doll's flat face or fine clothing made from leftover scraps that somehow captures the essence of an era. But like all folk art, the best handmade dolls radiate a spirit that goes beyond their humble beginnings.

Carousels

Folk art never develops in isolation. Folk art results from human responses to real needs. Some needs such as food, shelter, and clothing help people to survive. Other needs are more abstract. People need beauty in their lives. They need love. And, they need to have fun. In the late 19th century in Europe, the

GUSTAVE BAYOL, CAROUSEL CARVER

The most famous French carousel maker in the 19th century was Gustave Bayol, whose small carving shop turned out delicate animals carved with meticulous detail. Bayol was quite renowned for his carving skills and eventually hired many craftsmen to help in his factory. But Bayol never stopped carving. The book *Fairground Art* characterizes Bayol's unique style:

> His horses, whether galloping or standing on their hind legs are instantly recognizable. The curved neck tapers towards the toylike head. The expression is gentle with open eyes and upright ears. A strand of hair falls over the browband to hang down the horse's forehead and the tail is usually wooden. The harness is sometimes decorated with tassels, jewels, and rosettes.

Bayol eventually sold his factory in 1909 and purchased a small shop. There, dressed in a wide-brimmed hat and clogs, the man with a moustache and long hair continued to carve toys for children until his death in 1931.

Geoff Weedon and Richard Ward, *Fairground Art*. New York: Abbeville Press, 1981, p. 64.

economy changed from one based on farming to one based on manufacturing. As a result, populations in the cities grew, and people began having fun in new ways.

While families had always enjoyed the arrival in town of a traveling carnival or fair, the rapid growth of mass transportation in the 19th century changed the nature of the carnivals, too. Until then, small boys, horses, and donkeys propelled the roundabouts, or roughly carved wooden animals, in endless circles. But the steam engine could push much larger, heavier carved animals for longer rides. Furthermore, as the beasts grew larger, there was more space for the carvers' creativity. The animals that circled endlessly on the early roundabouts in England were carved to imitate nature as closely as possible. Carvers etched realistic shapes out of wood, and painters dappled the finished bodies with natural colors. Manes and tails were fashioned of real horsehair, which did not last long. Anxious children yanked it out as they climbed on their wooden steeds then hung on for dear life while their ponies circled. Many early carousel carvers were itinerant carpenters seeking extra income during the sparse winter months.

Charles J. Spooner was an English woodworker who began his carving business in the early 1900s by turning out rocking horses and pull toys. He soon became renowned for his ornate, galloping carousel horses. Their carved muscles, the angles of their heads and necks, and their ornate harnesses expressed speed and movement like no others. Spooner was especially recognized for the ornate saddles harnessed to his mounts with carved wooden straps.

Carousel production was rarely a one-person job. As businesses grew and demand increased, many artisans were needed to finish a job. Some carved legs, while others carved heads; some workers sanded, and others applied the paint. Usually, however, the master carver, or foreman, determined the details of each part. Geoff Weedon and Richard Ward, in their book *Fairground Art*, note that Spooner continued to influence the finished products of his factory in the English town Burton-on-Trent. They write,

> Even when Spooner himself no longer carved, the heads retained the same kindly expression. The eyes are open wide, the wooden ears point forward and the small, undershot jaw hangs open under a heavy muzzle. The cheek-piece curves from bit to head-piece, imitating the line of the plump jowl beneath."[34]

While he was not the only carousel maker to include animals other than horses, Spooner's reputation for creativity and innovation

was renowned. Roosters, swans, turkeys, pigs, donkeys, cows, goats, elephants, bears, lions, dragons, and ostriches all followed each other around and around on Spooner's carousels.

By the end of the 19th century, the modern carousel was off and running, first in Europe then in America, a land of opportunity for ambitious carvers, painters, musicians, and other artisans. In order to keep trolley lines and railroads profitable, large parks were constructed along the railway and at the end of the trolley lines, providing weekend destinations for entire families. These parks were also prime ground for the installation

This old-fashioned carousel has hand-carved, painted wooden animals. In modern times, carousel animals are most often made of plastic materials.

of permanent carousels, and since they were permanent, they could be larger and heavier. Also, overhead crank systems gave birth to "jumpers," animals that moved up and down a pole. Carvers indulged their creativity and carved magnificent beasts with flowing manes and bulging muscles. Charles Looff, an 18-year-old furniture maker who sailed to America from Germany, supplemented his income by giving dancing lessons and carving wooden animals in the evenings. He was a carver who took full advantage of the new carousel technology. As the authors of *Fairground Art* explain: "Given the opportunity to gallop, the horses reared and plunged, tossing their heads in a fury that sent their manes whipping about their heads."[35]

Three distinct styles of carousel carving developed in America: Philadelphia style, Coney Island style, and County Fair style. The animals on Philadelphia style carousels were large, strong, and tended to look the most realistic. In contrast, Coney Island style carousel animals were slender, with fanciful manes, and expressive faces. The saddles and other trappings were often studded with jewels. The smallest, lightest animals circled about on County Fair carousels, since they had to be taken apart frequently and moved from town to town.

The three styles shared certain features, however. For example, the figures on the outer row known as standers, are usually quite large and have three feet planted firmly on the ground. The animals on the inner rows, on the other hand, are smaller. They are either prancers, whose front legs are raised and whose back feet are planted on the platform, or jumpers, which go up and down on poles and have four bent legs. The side that faces onlookers is the "Romance side" and features the most elaborate carving and ornamentation. The side that few people see is often rather plain. Furthermore, European and Mexican carousels rotate counter-clockwise, while American carousels run in the opposite direction.

Carving carousel animals is a folk art that has mostly succumbed to modern technology and plastic. Some original carousels still operate in the United States, but it is hard to find craftsmen with the knowledge and skills to maintain them as they age. Still, it is a folk art that flourished at a time when many countries were rushing ahead with new ideas and pouring creative energy into new ways of making money and having a good time.

Whirligigs and Other Toys that Move

While carousels were popular, they were hardly portable. Immigrant families brought small toys to America tucked into tiny spaces to entertain their children. And if the actual toys did not fit in the trunk, the idea for the toy was readily stored in the memories of parents to be taken out and assembled as soon as possible. The United States became a toy melting pot of sorts where toys from Ireland, China, France, Germany, England, Africa, Mexico, and every other country mingled, combining certain qualities and developing in unique ways. Folk toys that could be pulled on wheels, spun like tops, or operated by air and wind were among the most popular.

Whirligigs, for example, were brought to this country by Pennsylvania Germans and probably developed from weather-vanes, since they operated in the same way. Made purely for entertainment, the opposing arms of simple whirligigs spun round and round, modeled after the common windmill. With a few cuts of the knife and some paint, those spinning arms became a policeman, a soldier, or a housewife accomplishing one of her many household chores, such as doing the laundry, churning butter, milking a cow, or chopping wood. With the addition of gears, multiple figures accomplished several tasks at once, the same breeze powering the entire mechanism. And of course, the faster the wind blew, the more furiously the whirligig accomplished its tasks.

Moving air also powered other folk toys. Breezes carry kites aloft to amuse both children and adults, while displaying their magnificent colors and shapes. Another folk toy called a pipsqueak made sounds when air was squeezed through a small bellows, such as those of an accordion. When the bellows were squeezed, sheep said, "baa," cows said, "moo," and ducks quacked. Some pipsqueaks flapped their wings or moved their tiny tongues in and out of their mouths along with mimicking the sounds of animals.

Pull toys also came in several versions. Sometimes a toy was simply mounted on a wheeled platform and pulled around. Not content with simplicity, however, more ambitious craftsmen connected wires or strings from the wheels to moving parts on the toy that would then move up and down or back and forth as the wheels turned.

Other mechanisms powered toys, too. Propelled only by a weighted ball suspended from the toy by a string that swings back and forth, a simple carved wooden trio of musicians from Russia plays the lute and dances. Even more primitive, the limberjack, which originated in Ireland, dances and swings its wooden arms and legs as it bumps lightly against a small board that is tapped by hand in rhythm to music. Musical Tete Jumeau dolls from France were powered by internal wind-up mechanisms that made them dance and sing. Yo-yos, thought to have originated in China are powered only by gravity and spinning, or centrifugal, force.

Folk toys, whether simple or complex, embody what is most enduring about childhood: imagination, an innocent world in which creativity still reigns. Though electronic gadgets are inviting, folk toys never go out of style. As John R. Nelson says, "Folk toys are still with us and in use after all the bells and whistles of many contemporary designs have fallen silent. The strong, simple, homemade toy goes on, waiting to be picked up and played with."[36] Like all folk art, the materials may change, but the basic impulses never do. Whenever a child picks something up and invests it with his or her own imagination, the spirit of folk art lives on.

Notes

Introduction: Diverse Art with Common Features

1. Marion Oettinger, Jr., *The Folk Art of Latin America*. New York: Dutton Studio Books, 1992, p. 94.

Chapter One: The Roots of Folk Art

2. Stacy C. Hollander and Brooke Davis Anderson, *American Anthem, Masterworks from the American Folk Art Museum*. New York: Harry N. Abrams, 2001, p. 20.
3. Robert Bishop and Jacqueline M. Atkins, *Folk Art in American Life*. New York: Viking Studio Books, 1995, p. 3.
4. Ann Oppenheimer, "16 Years, a History of the Folk Art Society," *Folk Art Messenger*, http://www.folkart.org/about/about.html.
5. *American Anthem*, p.16.
6. *Folk Art in American Life*, p. 1.
7. Carl Lindquist, "Chandigarh and the Rock Garden," http://www.clt.astate.edu/elind/nc_main.htm.

Chapter Two: Useful Objects of Everyday Life

8. Tsune Sugimura, *The Enduring Crafts of Japan*. New York: Walker/Weatherhill, 1968, p. 24.
9. *Kindred Spirits*, catalog of the Mingei International Museum of World Folk Art. San Diego, 1995, p. 11.
10. Rebecca Sawyer-Fay, *Living with Folk Art*. New York: Hearst Books, 1994, p. 44.
11. *Living with Folk Art*, p. 118.
12. *Living with Folk Art*. p. 104.

Chapter Three: Ready-to-Wear

13. Lucy Davies and Mo Fini, *Arts and Crafts of South America*. San Francisco: Chronicle Books, 1994, p. 8.
14. *Arts and Crafts of South America*, p. 57.
15. *Arts and Crafts of South America*, p. 71.
16. National Museum of African Art, "Wrapped in Pride," http://www.nmafa.si.edu/exhibits/kente/top.htm.

17. Victor and Takako Hauge, *Folk Traditions in Japanese Art*. Tokyo: Kodansha International Ltd. 1978, p. 26.

18 Quoted in Ogawa Masataka, *The Enduring Crafts of Japan*. New York: Walker/Weatherhill, 1968, p. 60.

19. *The Enduring Crafts of Japan*, p. 74.

Chapter Four: Decorating Inside and Out

20. Quoted in Sumpter Priddy, *American Fancy*. Milwaukee: Chipstone Foundation, 2004, p. 125.

21. *Living with Folk Art*, p. 143.

22. Mary Ellisor Emmerling, *Collecting American Country*. New York: Clarkson N. Potter, Inc., 1983, p. 28.

23. Trond Gjerdi, "Norwegian Folk Art," Bergen Guide. http://www.bergen-guide.com/404.htm.

24. Quoted in *The Enduring Crafts of Japan*, p. 126.

Chapter Five: Celebration and Ritual

25. Roman Black, *Old and New Australian Aboriginal Art*. Australia: Angus & Robertson Ltd., 1964, p. 65.

26. Manataka American Indian Council, "Totem Poles of the Great Northwest," http://www.manataka. org/page30.html.

27. Barton Wright, *Hopi Kachinas*. Flagstaff: Northland Publishing, 1977, p. 22.

28. *Hopi Kachinas*, p. 2.

29. Marion Oettinger, Jr., *The Folk Art of Latin America*. New York: Dutton Studio Books, 1992, p. 38.

Chapter Six: Dolls, Carousels, and Other Amusements

30. Bradley Smith, *First Collections, Dolls and Folk Toys of the World*. La Jolla: Mingei International Museum of World Folk Art, 1987, p. 20.

31. Wendy Lavitt, *American Folk Dolls*. New York: Alfred A. Knopf, Inc.,1982, p. 4.

32. *American Folk Dolls*, p. 70.

33. *American Folk Dolls*, p. 96

34. Geoff Weedon and Richard Ward, *Fairground Art*. New York: Abbeville Press, 1981, p. 28.

35. *Fairground Art*, p. 75.

36. John R. Nelson, *American Folk Toys, Easy-to-Build Toys for All Ages*. Newtown, CT: Taunton Press, 1998, p. 20.

For Further Reading

Books

Lillian Ackerman, *A Song to the Creator: Traditional Arts of Native American Women of the Plateau.* Norman: University of Oklahoma Press, 1996. Explores traditional arts of the Plateau including storytelling, basket weaving, hide working, embroidery, and music. Beautiful photographs and black-and-white illustrations show the range of geometric and representational designs that these Native American groups incorporate into their arts.

Eleanor Coerr, *Sadako and the Thousand Paper Cranes.* New York: Puffin Books, 1977. This is the true story of Hiroshima-born Sadako who became ill from the effects of the atom bomb after it was dropped on her city in 1945. Describes Sadako's courage and her determination to fold one thousand origami cranes in her wish to recover.

Yvonne Merrill, *Hands-On Africa.* Salt Lake City: KITS Publishing, 2000. This Hands-On series is a beautifully illustrated introduction to folk art around the world. Each volume (Alaska, 1996), (Asia, 1999), (Celebrations, 1996), (Latin America, 1998), (Rocky Mountains, 1997), (Colonial America, African American,

Southeast American Indians, 2006) contains color photographs and easy-to-follow instructions for making folk art from the region.

John A. Nelson, *Folk Art Weathervanes.* Mechanicsburg: Stackpole Books, 1990. This book includes a brief history of weathervanes and sixty-eight patterns with complete instructions for making your own. Includes patterns for various fish and whales, horses, birds, ships, and trains.

John R. Nelson, *American Folk Toys.* Newtown: The Taunton Press, 1998. This book includes a cultural history of American folk toys and instructions for making many traditional toys, including a Jack-in-the-box, folk yo-yo, and Jacob's Ladder. Most projects require adult help, since they require the use of sharp tools.

Marion Oettinger, Jr. *The Folk Art of Latin America.* New York: Dutton Studio Books, 1992. This book, written by the curator of folk art and Latin American Art at the San Antonio Museum of Art, is a comprehensive exploration of many of the folk arts of Latin America, including ceremonial folk art, utilitarian folk art, recreational, and decorative folk art.

Richard Panchyk, *American Folk Art for Kids*. A good introduction to folk art that includes a brief overview plus several captivating activities including making a gum wrapper chain, painting a folk portrait, and making a rag doll.

James Haywood Rolling, Jr., *Come Look With Me: Discovering African American Art for Children*. New York: Lickle Publishing Inc., 2005. Examines twelve paintings by African American artists and engages students through questions to understand the unique struggles and contributions of these artists to the overall culture of the United States.

Florence Temko, *Traditional Crafts from the Caribbean*. Minneapolis: Lerner Publications Co., 2001.
Traditional Crafts from Africa (1996).
Traditional Crafts from China (2000).
Traditional Crafts from Japan (2000).
Traditional Crafts from Mexico and Central America (1996).
Traditional Crafts from Native North America (1997).

This series introduces the folk art of each region with user-friendly activities and just enough information to provide a good overall background about the region's art and history.

Li Xiaoxiang, *Origins of Chinese Folk Arts*. Singapore: Asiapac Books, 2002. This book written in comic book style explores the origins of Chinese embroidery, lacquer ware, paper cutting, masks, and pottery, as well as examines the Chinese connections to football, spinning tops, and swing sets.

Web sites

Akan Cultural Symbols Project (www.marshall.edu/akanart) This site contains beautiful photographs and descriptions of the art of Akan people of Ghana and Cote d'Ivoire. It includes detailed information about kente cloth, adinkra symbolism and stamping, and links to other arts such as pottery, metal casting, and woodcarving.

American Folk Art Museum (http://www.folkartmuseum.org) The Museum's website is an ongoing guide to current exhibitions. Also has some general information about folk art.

The American Folklife Center at the Library of Congress (http://www.loc.gov/folklife/edresources/index.html) This government site is an excellent resource for teachers and students interested in pursuing information about folk art from around the world. Various links guide students to lists of publications, activities, archives, recordings, and ongoing projects such as Storycorps, Save our Sounds, and the Veteran's History Project.

Interesting Ideas (http://www.interestingideas.com) This website is an interesting and amusing guide to many varieties of roadside art, outsider art, amd eccentric art. It is fun to get lost in its many links.

International Quilt Study Center at the University of Nebraska-Lincoln (www.quiltstudy.org) This website is an excellent way to access the ongoing work at the Quilt Study Center, which was established in 1997 to encourage the interdisciplinary study of all aspects of quilt making. Its mission is to collect, preserve, study, and promote the discovery of quilts and quilt making traditions from many cultures, countries, and time periods. It is also possible to subscribe to their free online quilt-of-the-month club.

Mingei International Museum of World Folk Art (www.mingei.org) Provides a guide to ongoing exhibitions at this museum in San Diego, California.

Videos

Full Circle Videos: Native American Art, Culture, and Music (www.fullcir.com) This company produces several series including a how-to series that includes instructions on making moccasins, beading, and dance shawls. Their Native American Masters series focus on outstanding craftsman such as Georgeann Robinson, an Osage Indian ribbonworker who was honored by the Smithsonian Institution; a Kiowa Indian cradleboard maker; and a Cherokee basketmaker.

Index

Picture Credits

About the Author

Tina Kafka lives in San Diego, California. This is her third book for Lucent Books. Her book *DNA on Trial* (Hot Topics) was awarded a San Diego Book Award for Children's and Young Adult's Non-fiction in 2004.

SCHOOL
olet Rd